NrdyLatinQueen Arts Presents:

An Amazing Beautiful Hand-Drawn Coloring Book

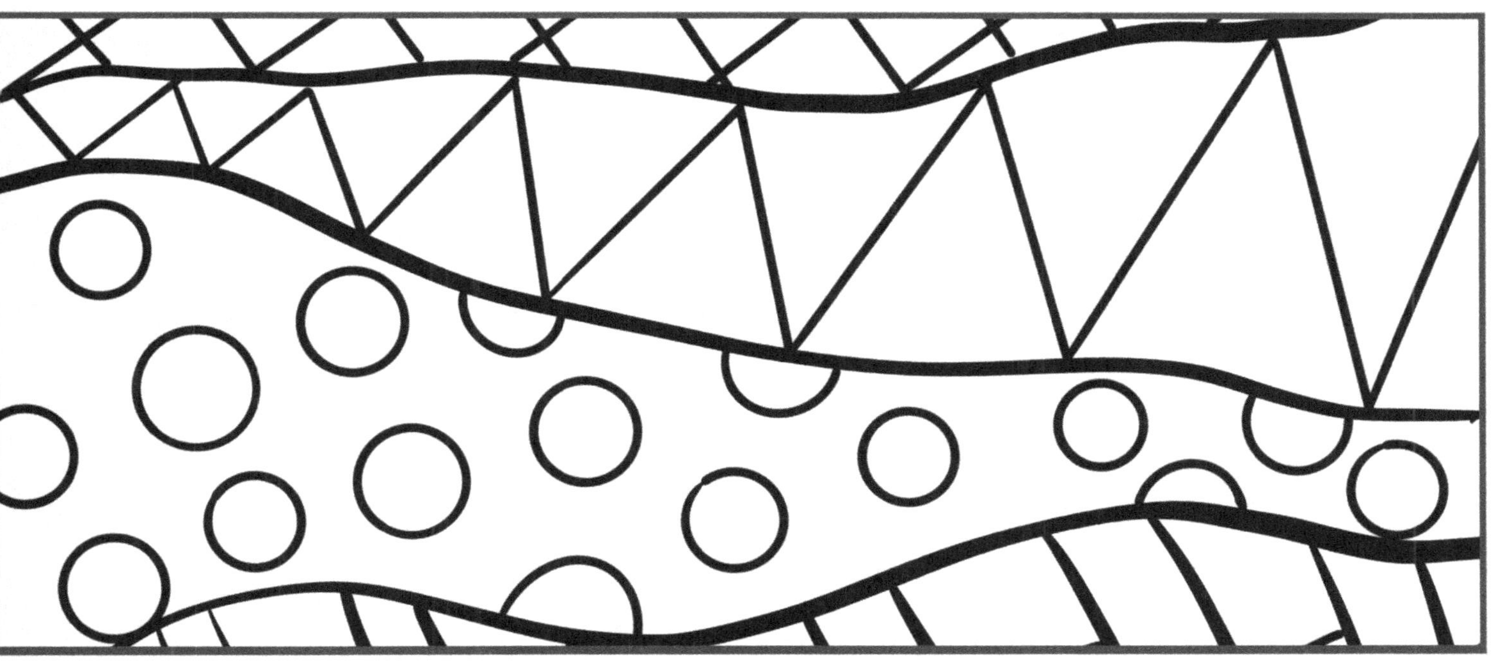

NrdyLatinQueen.com

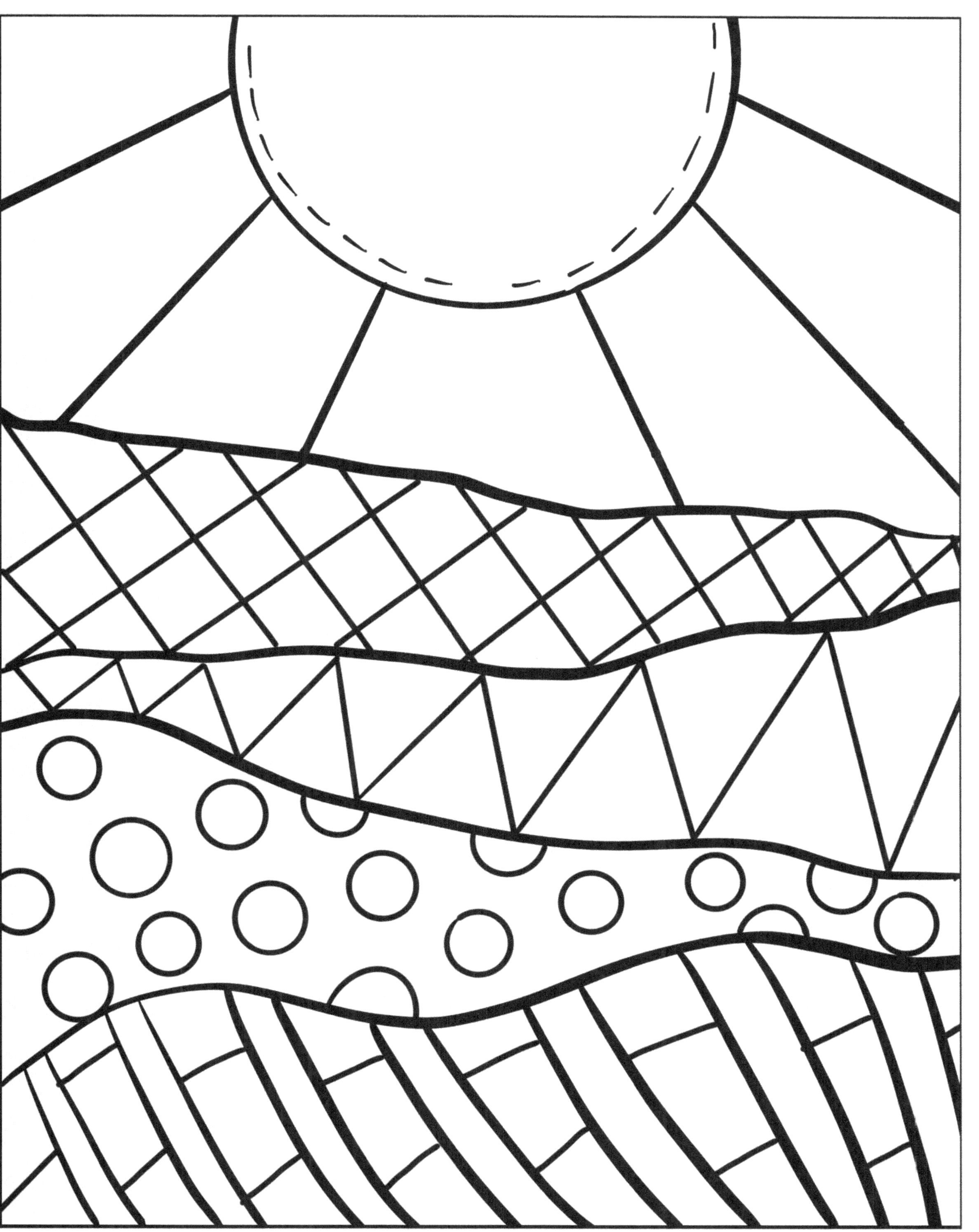

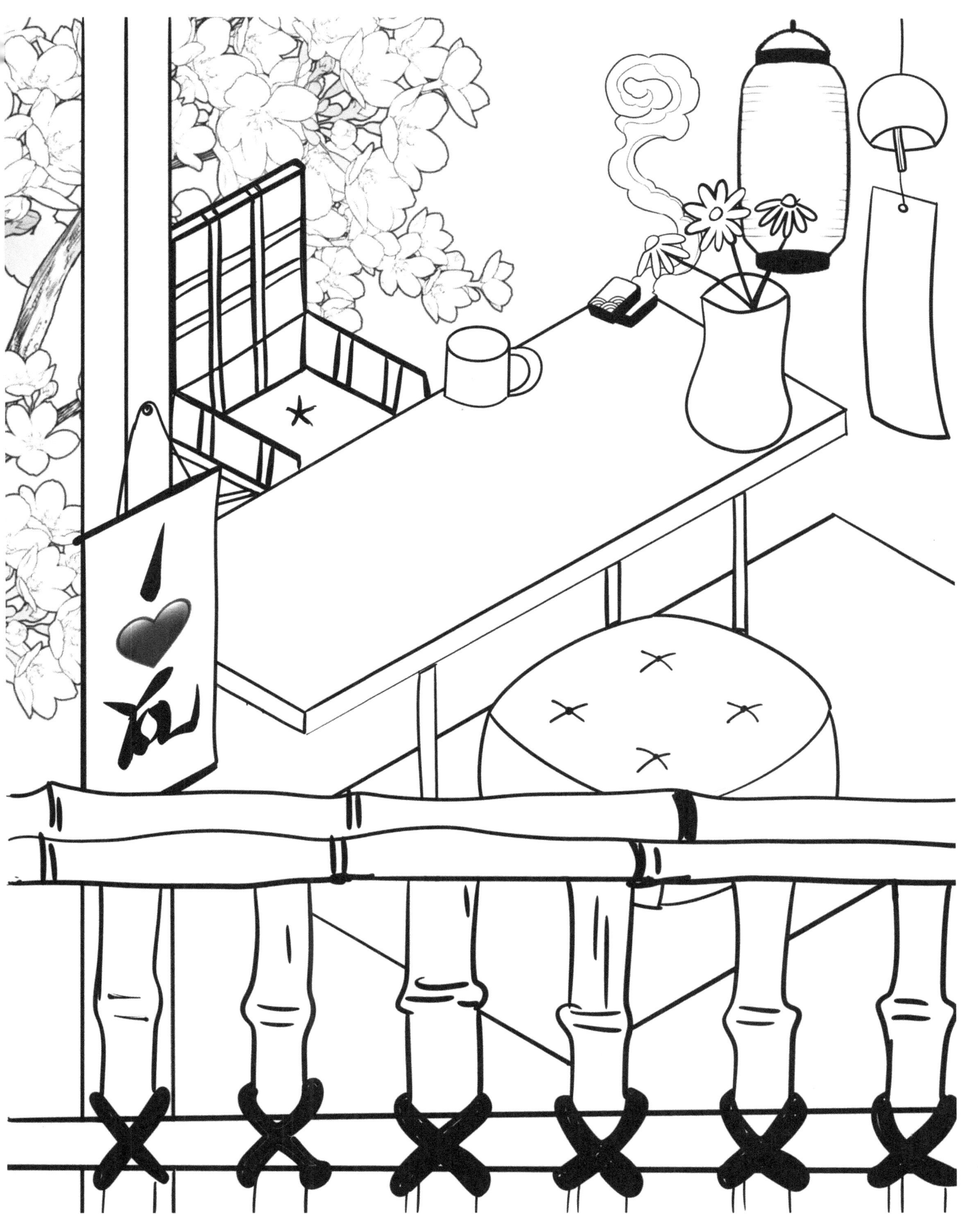
I ♥ YOU

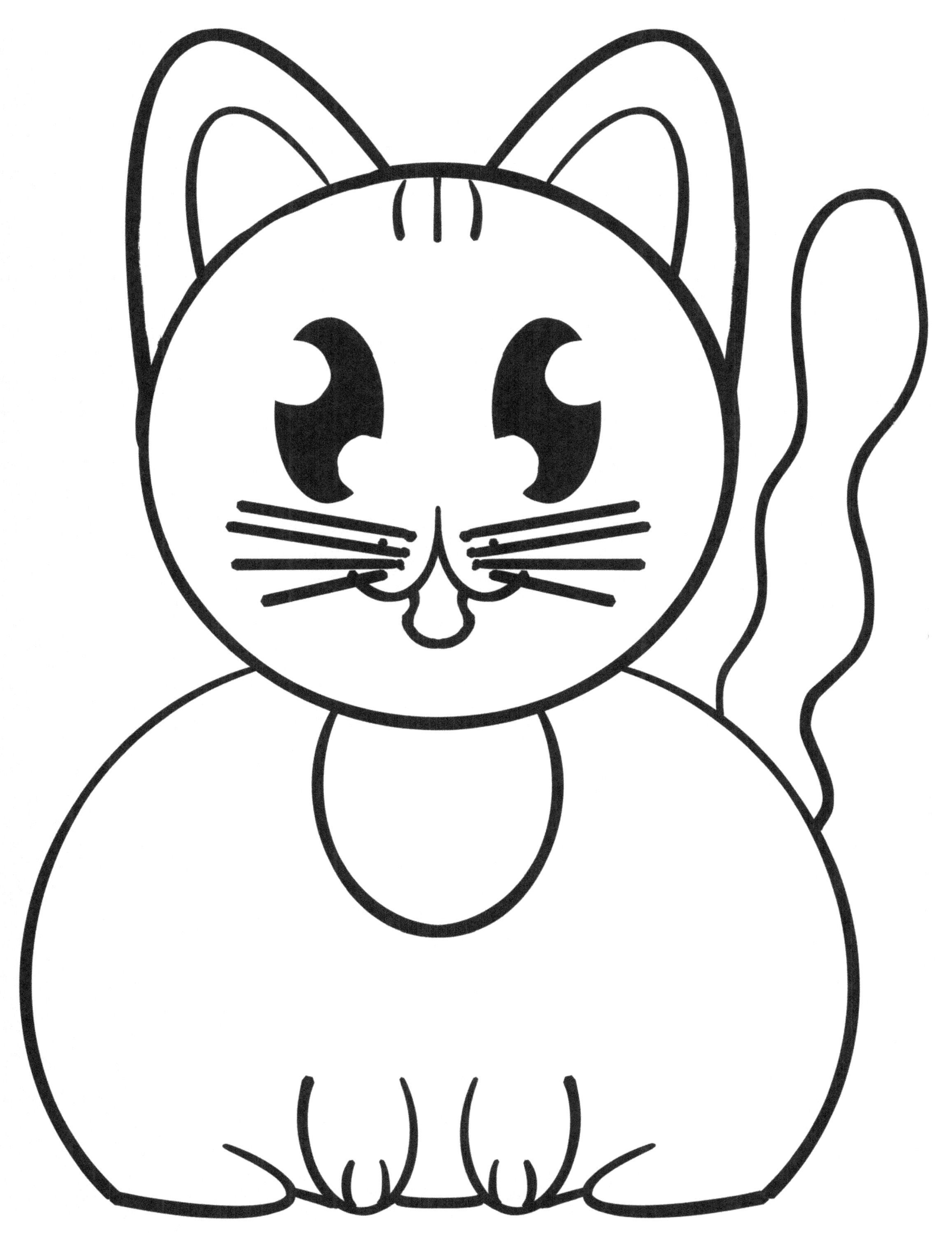

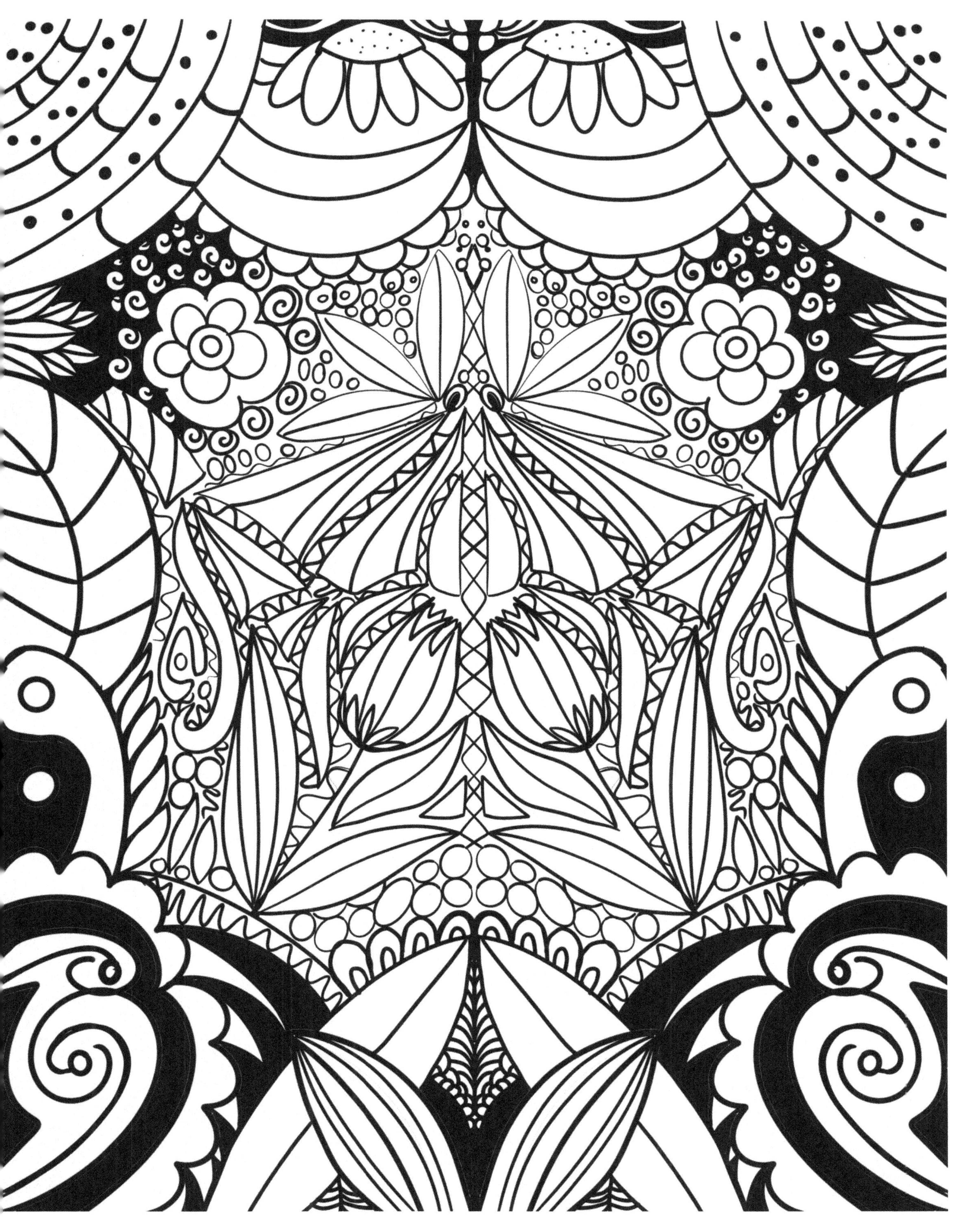

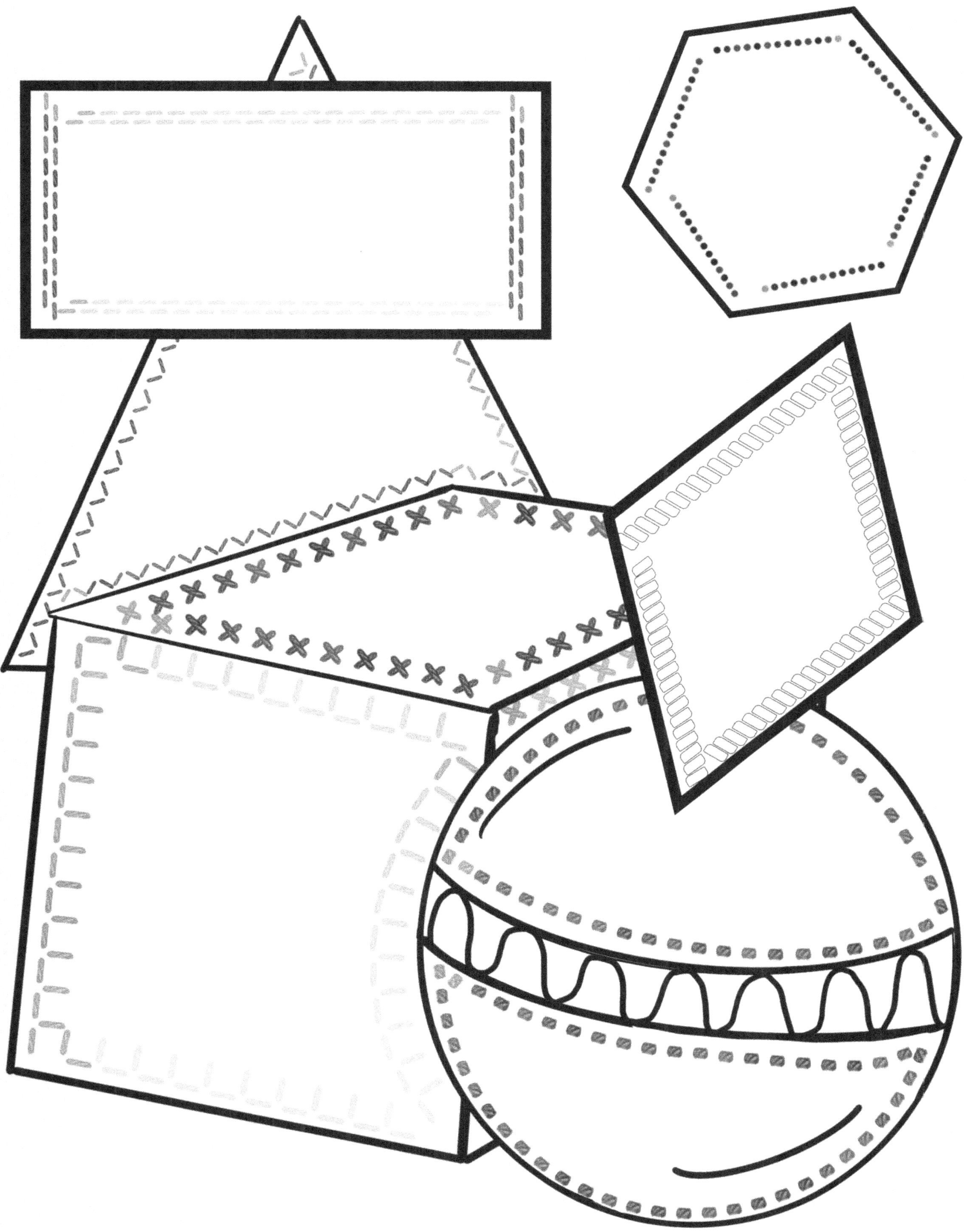

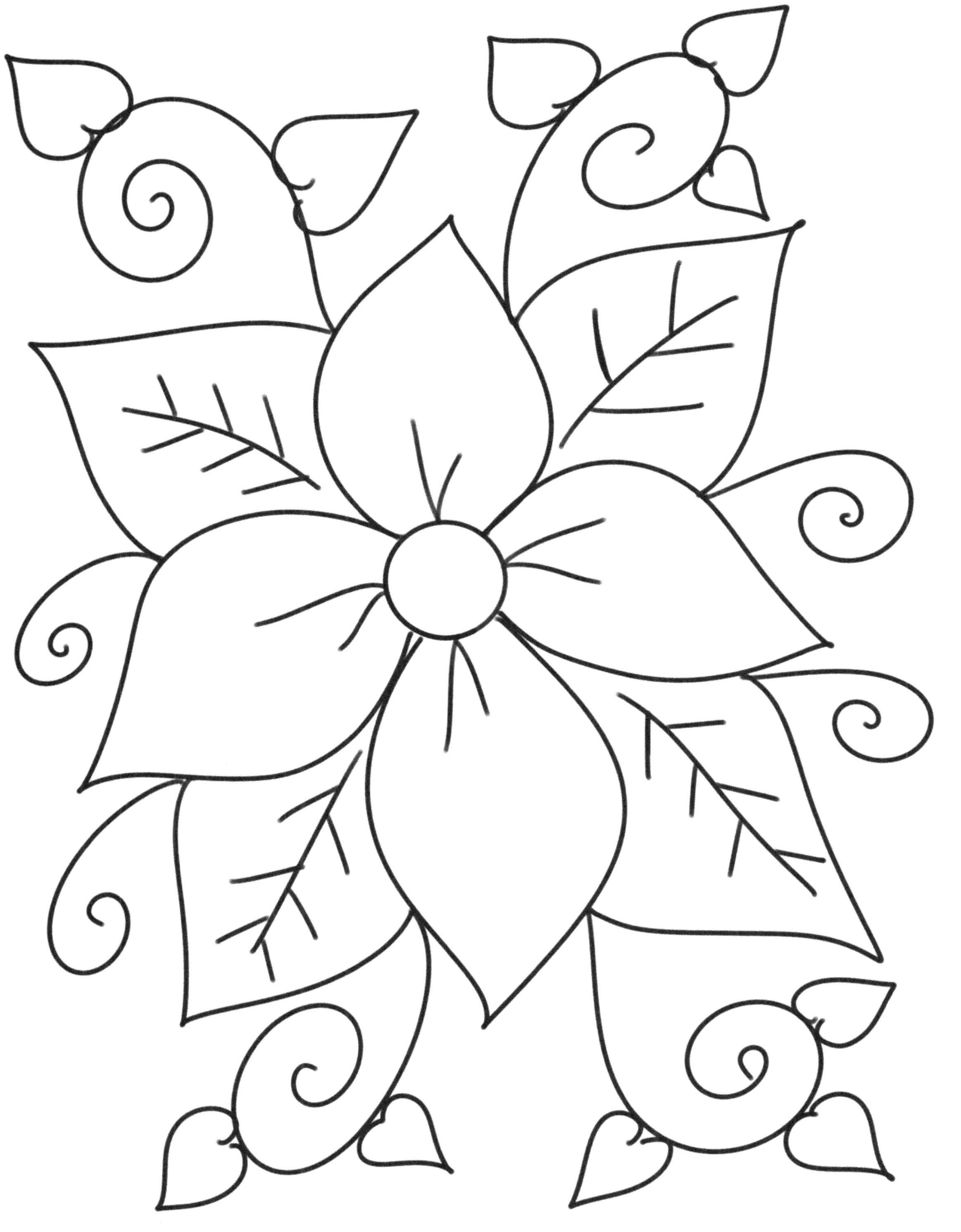

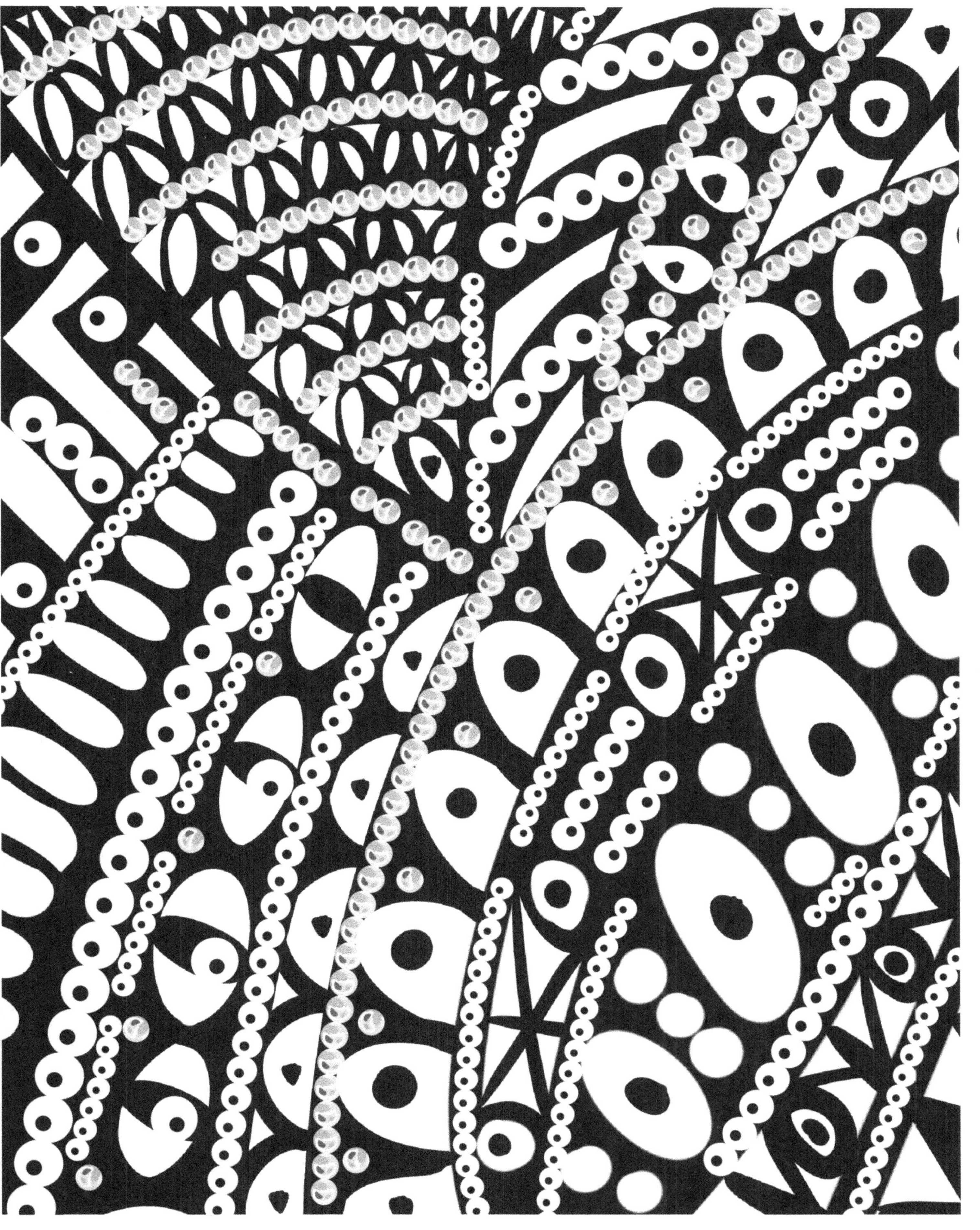

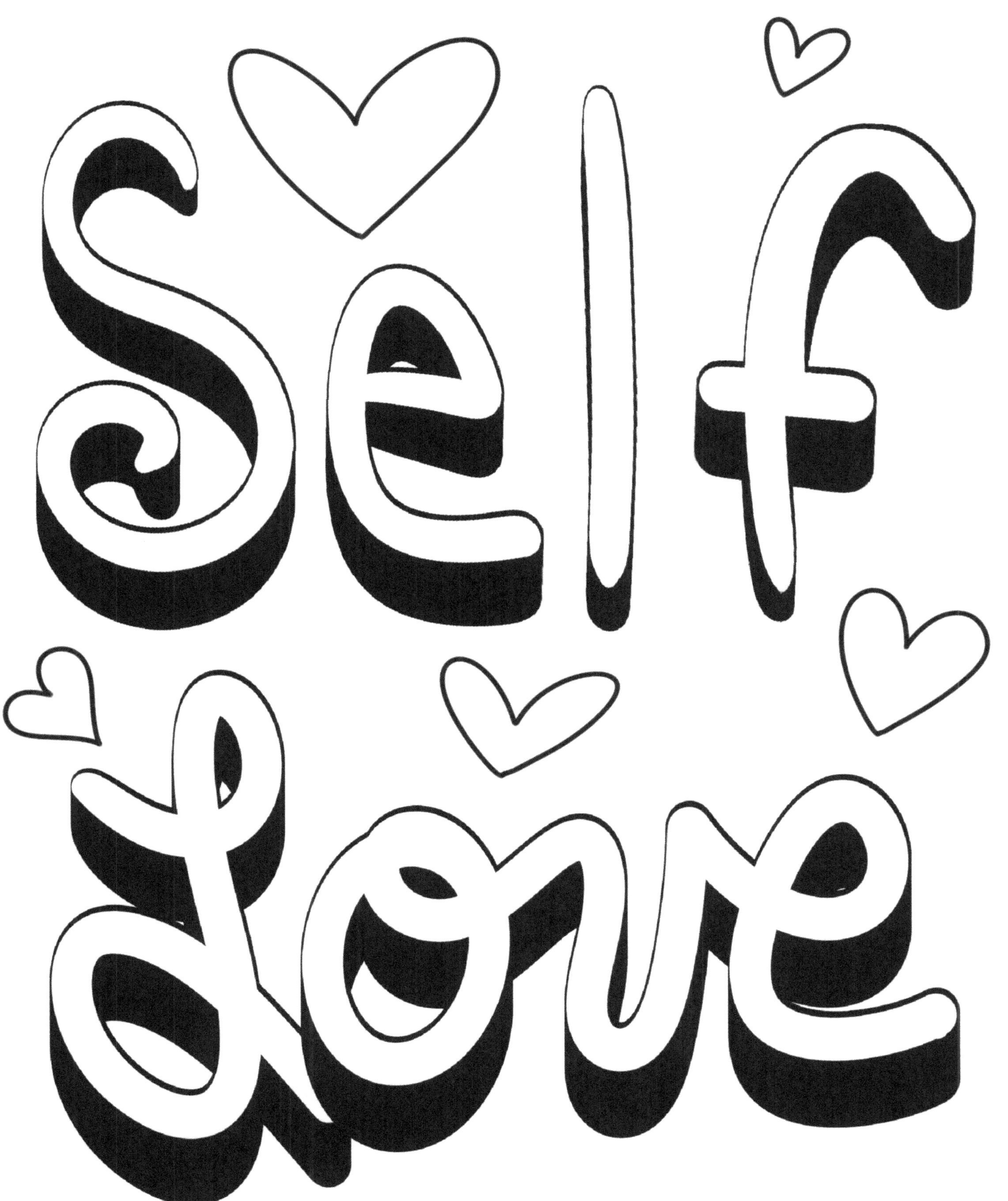
Self
love

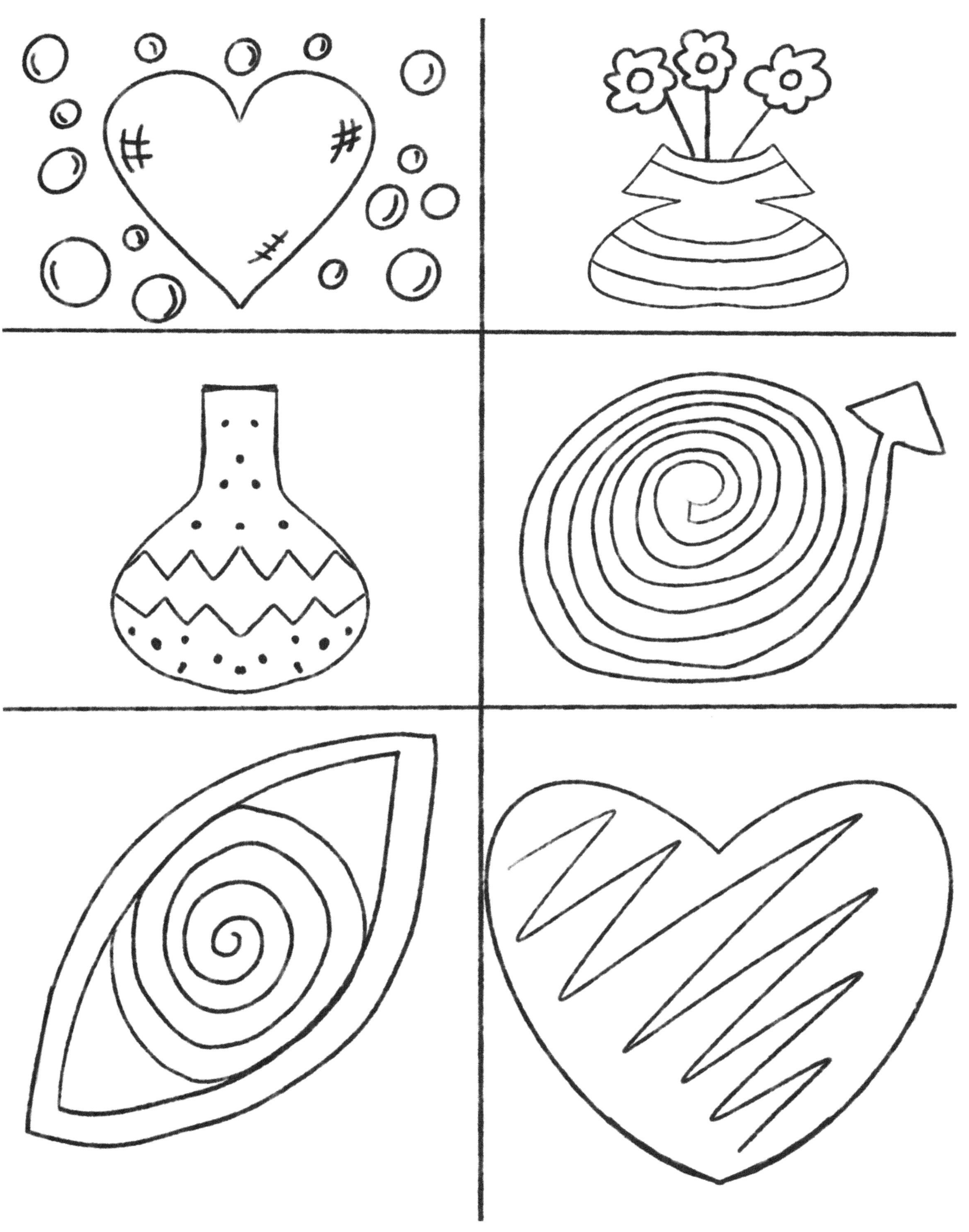

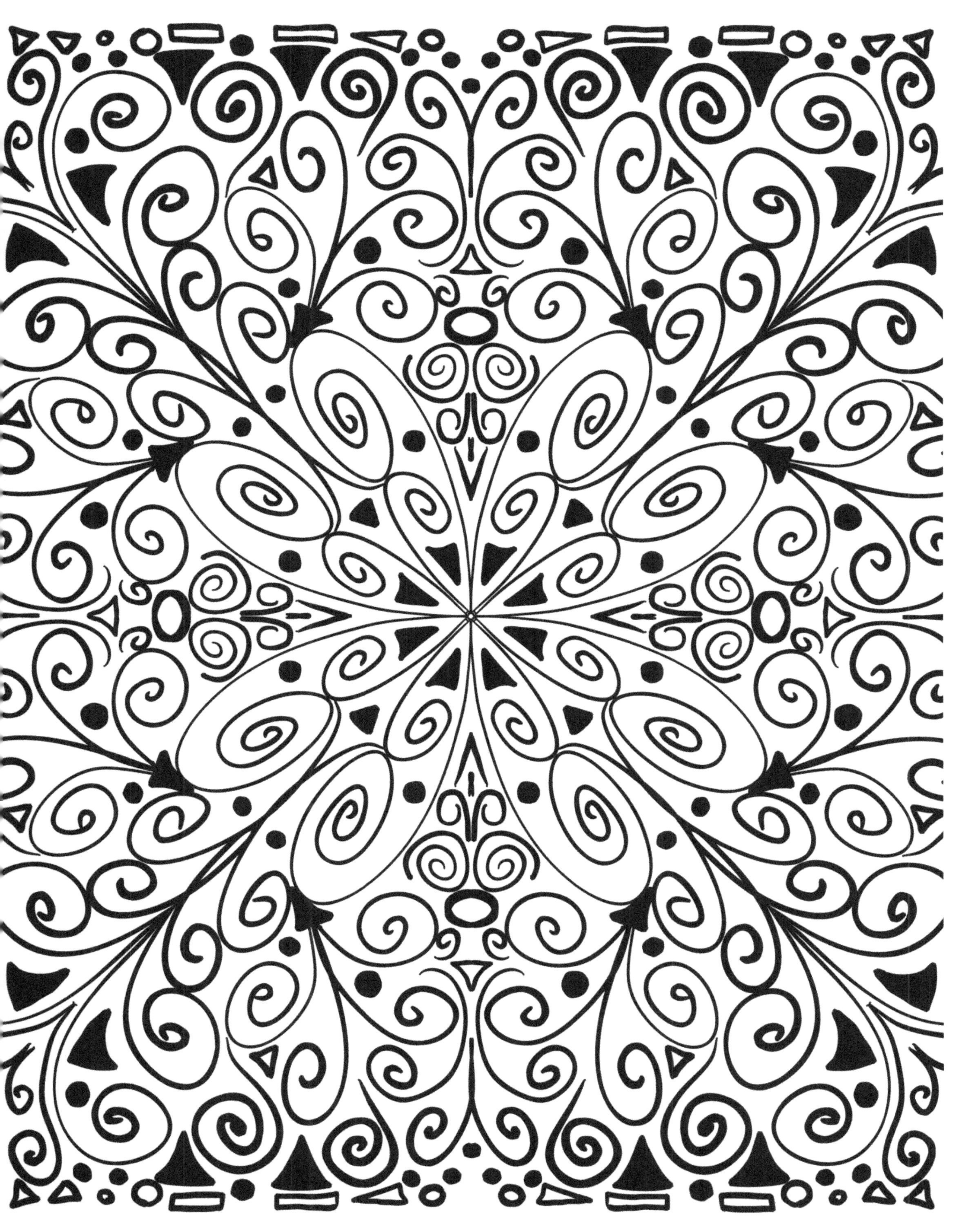

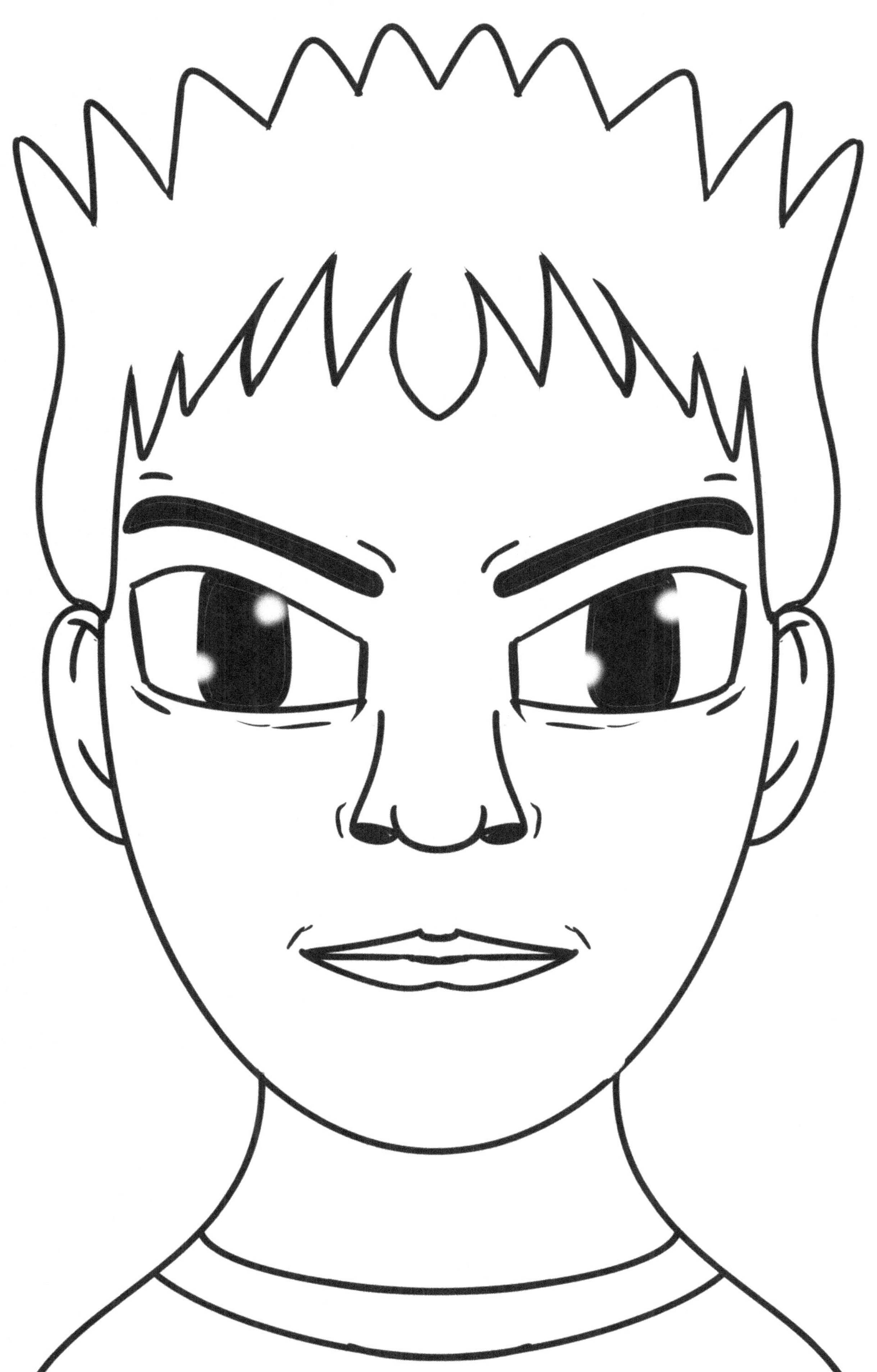

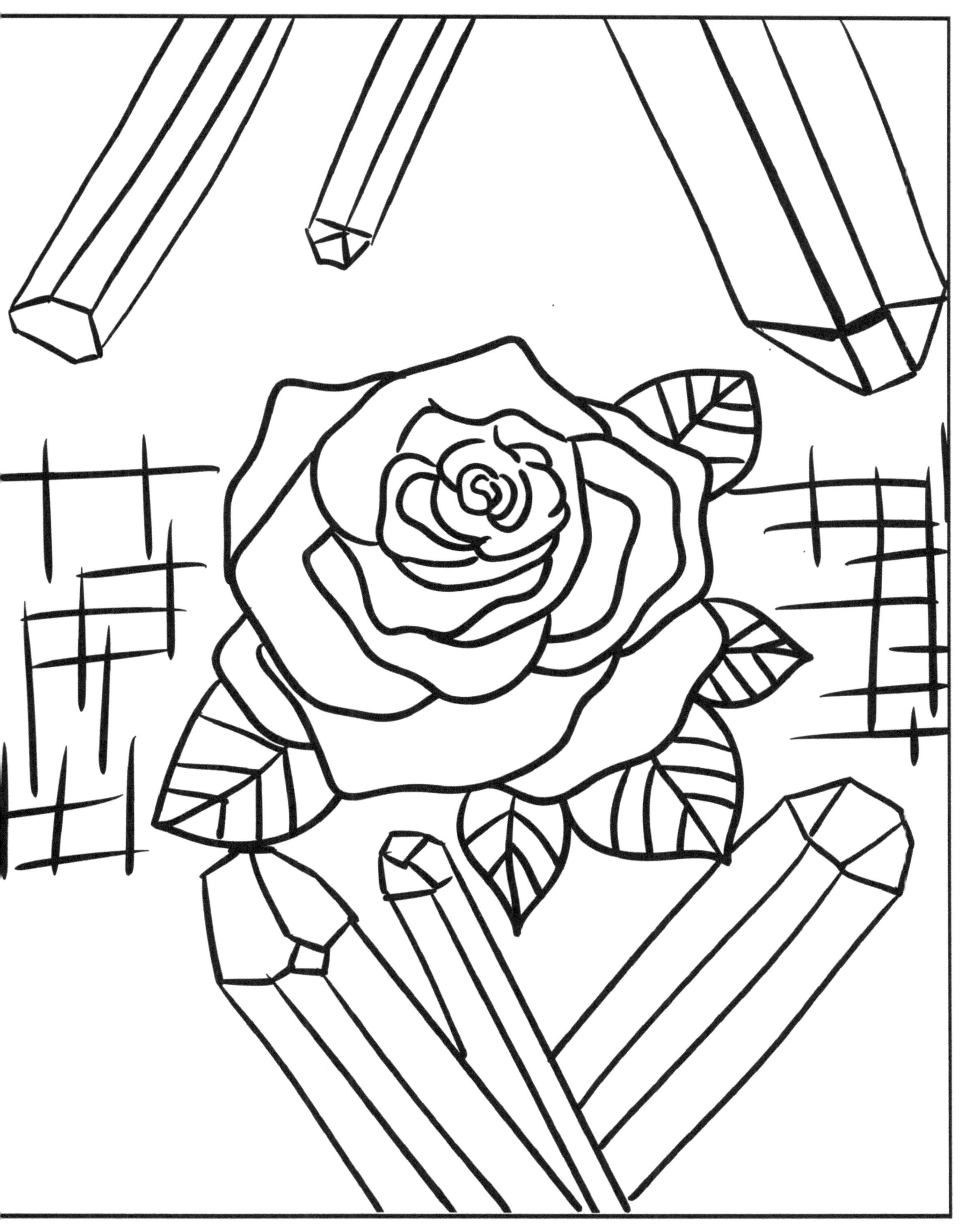

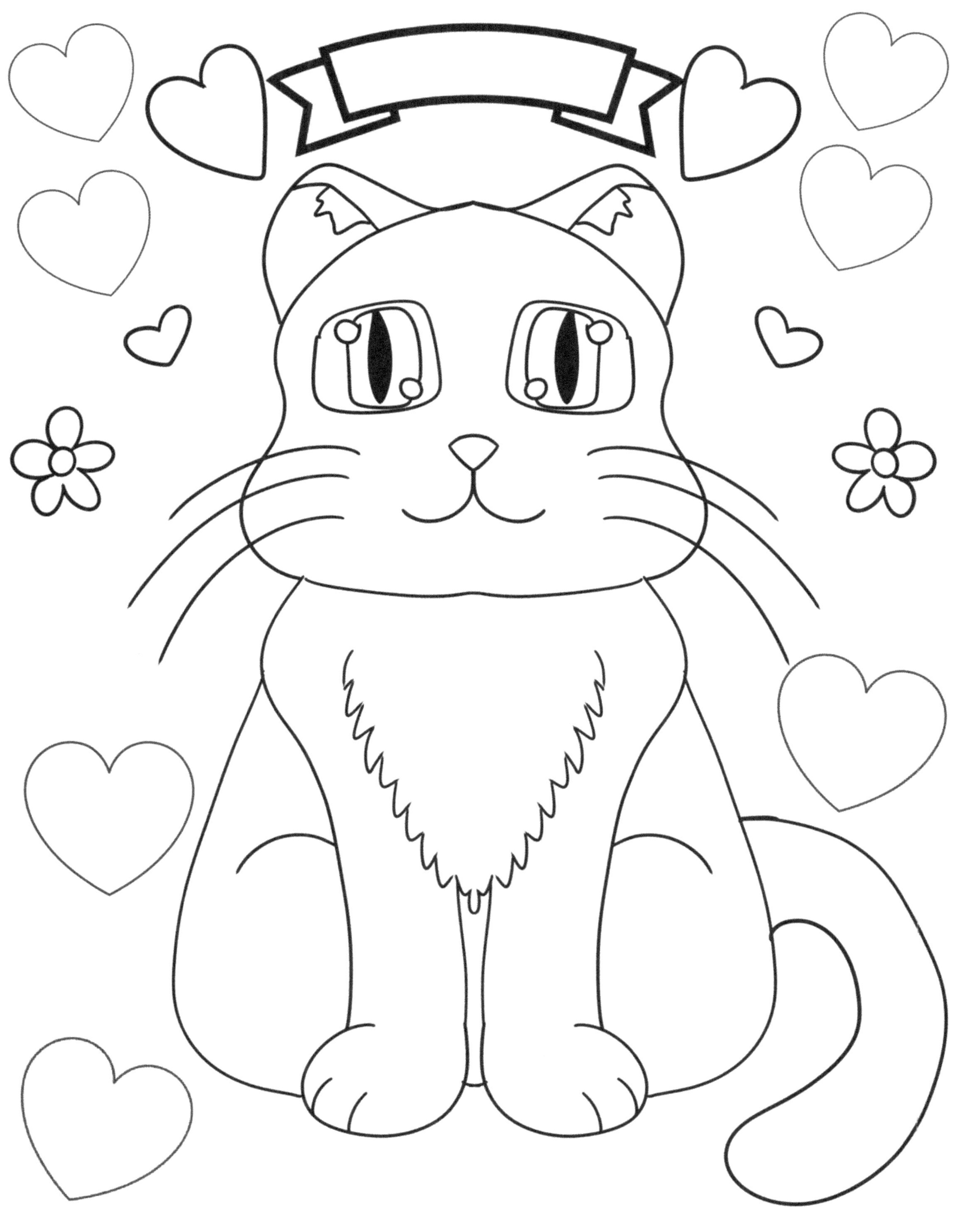

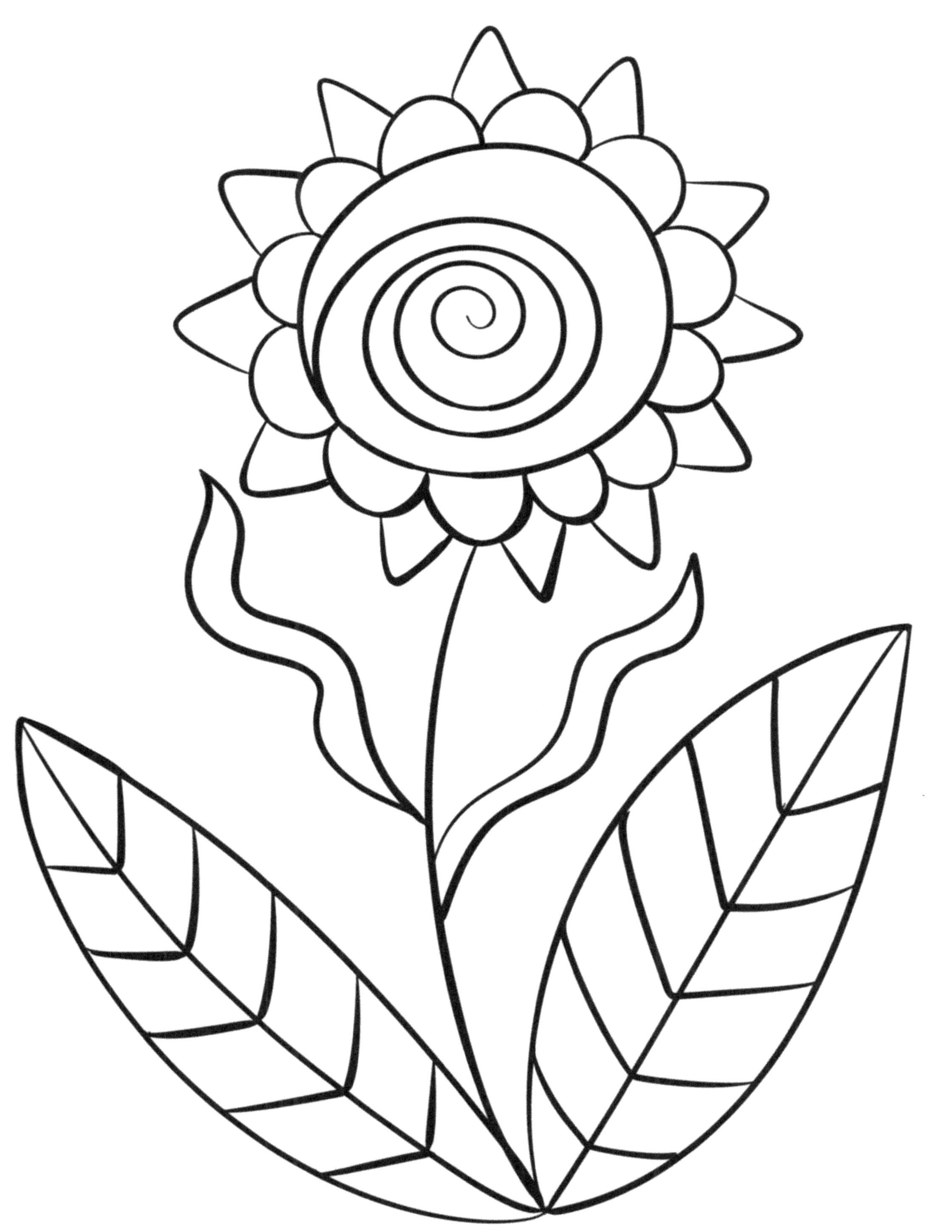

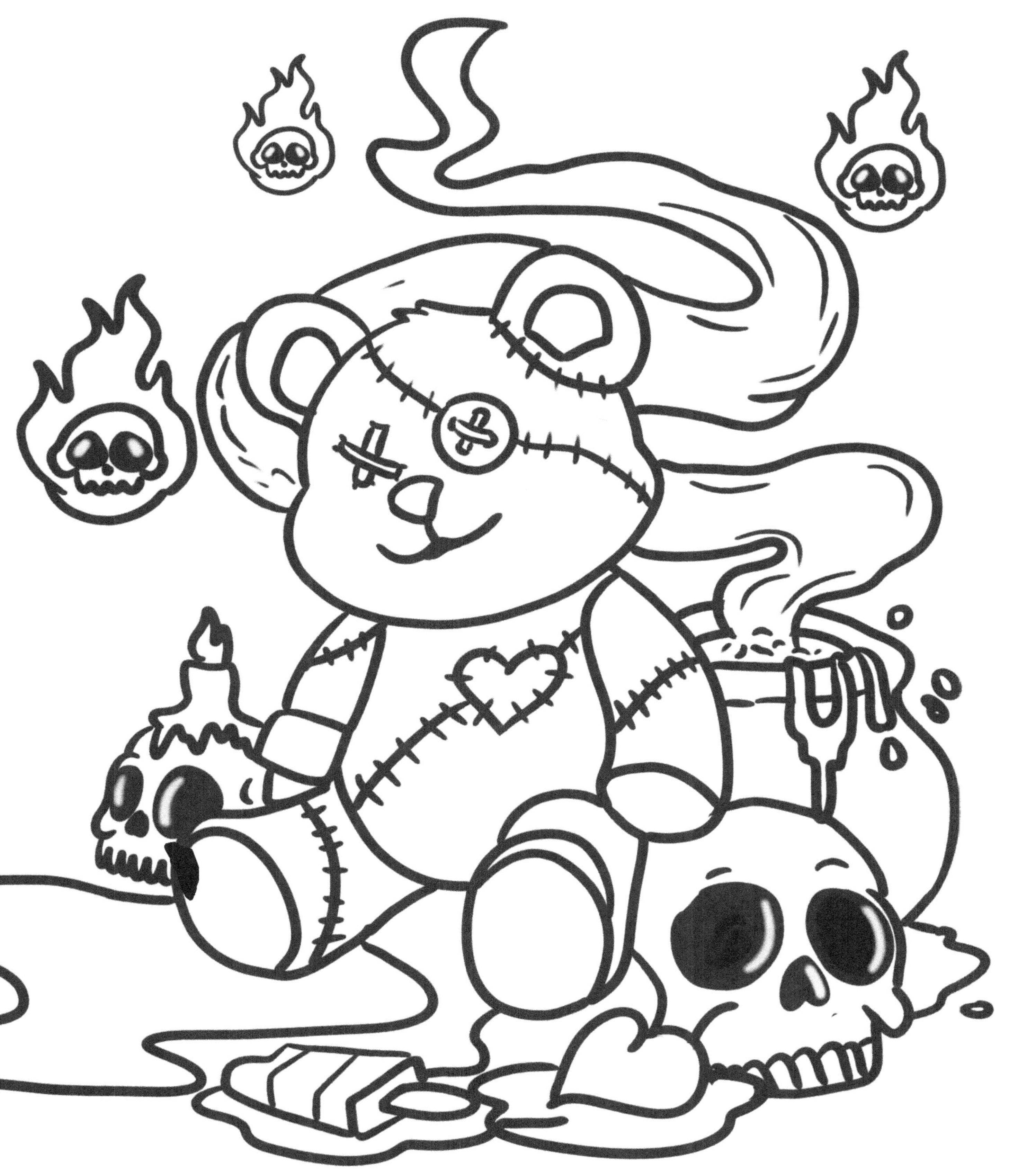

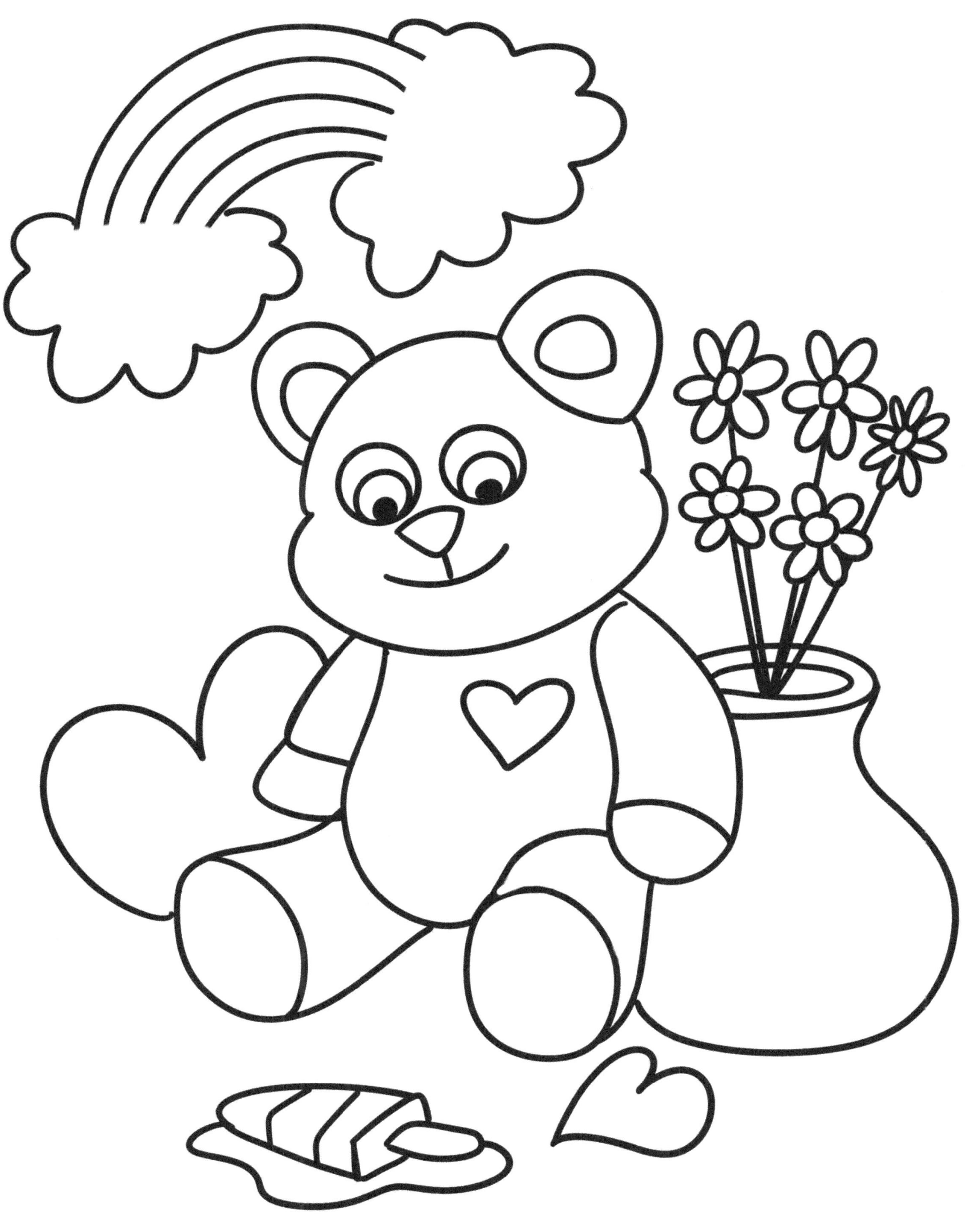

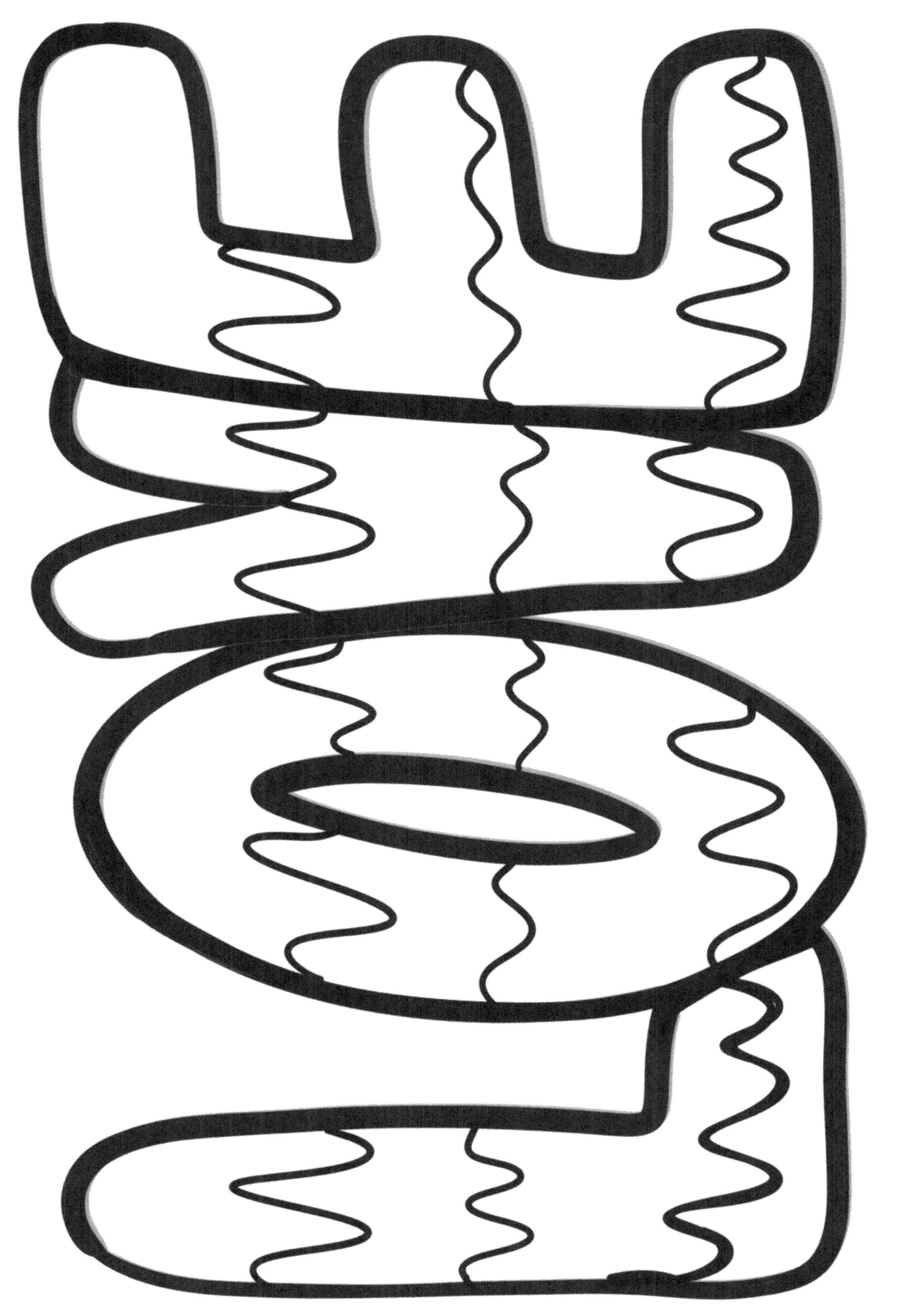

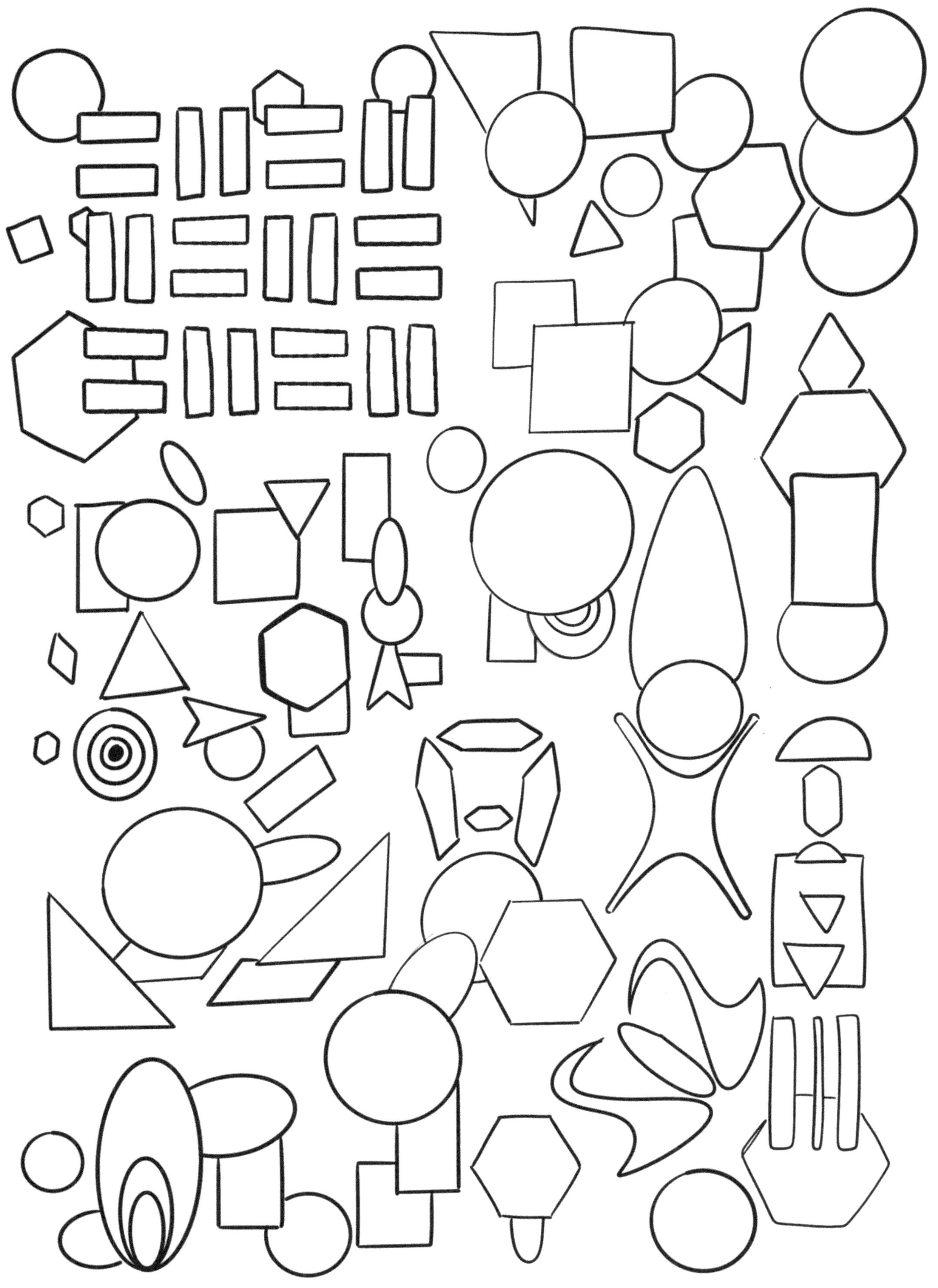

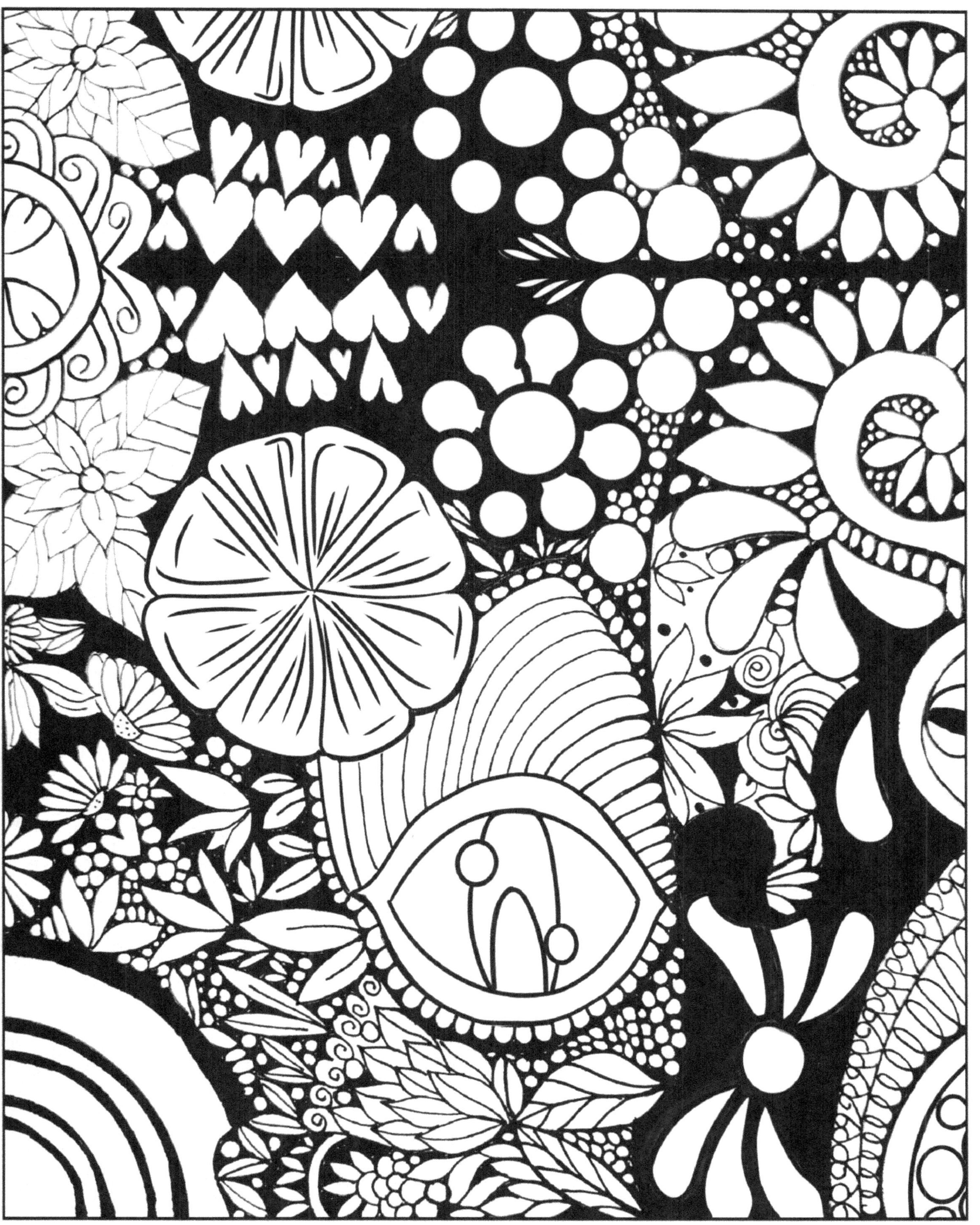

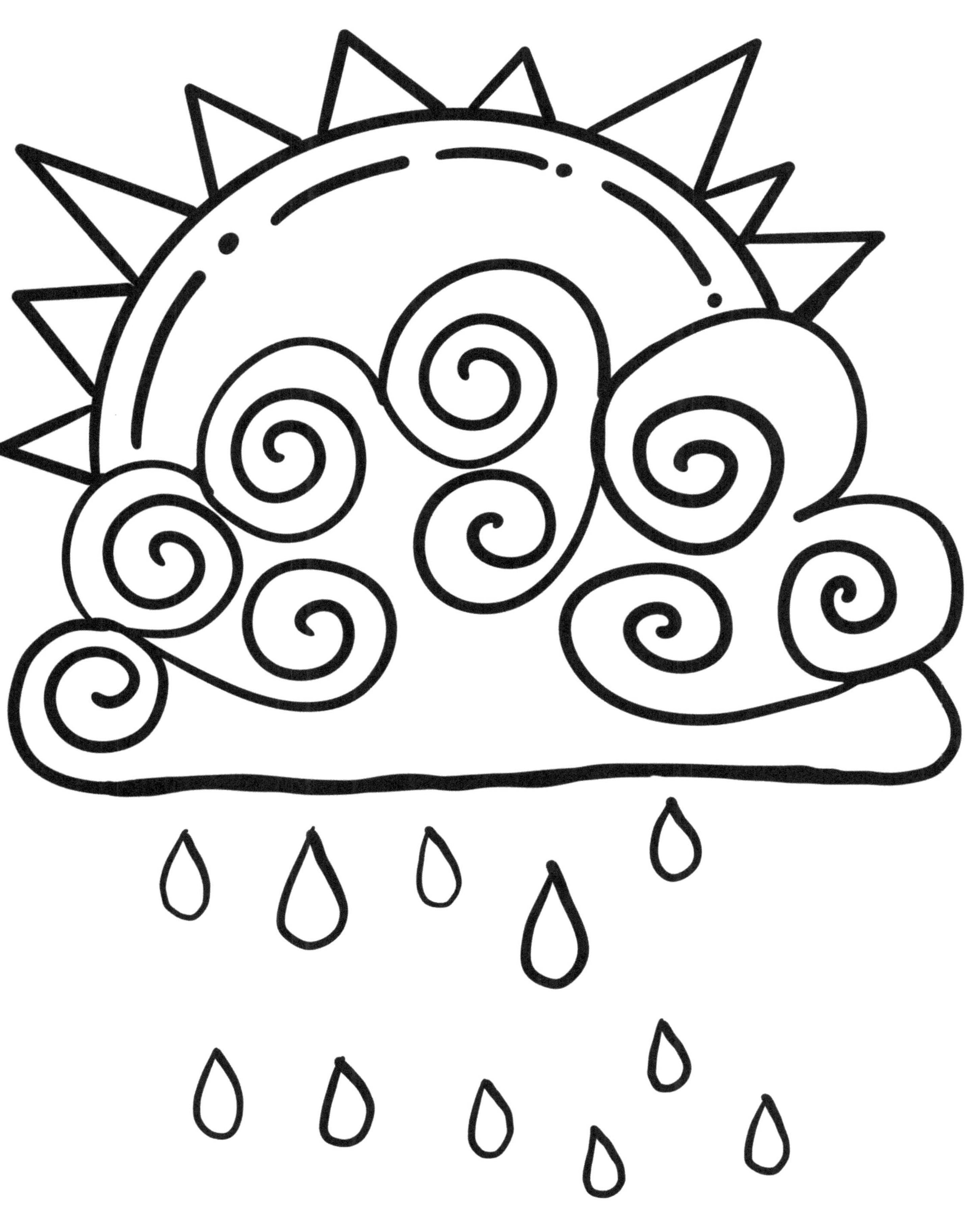

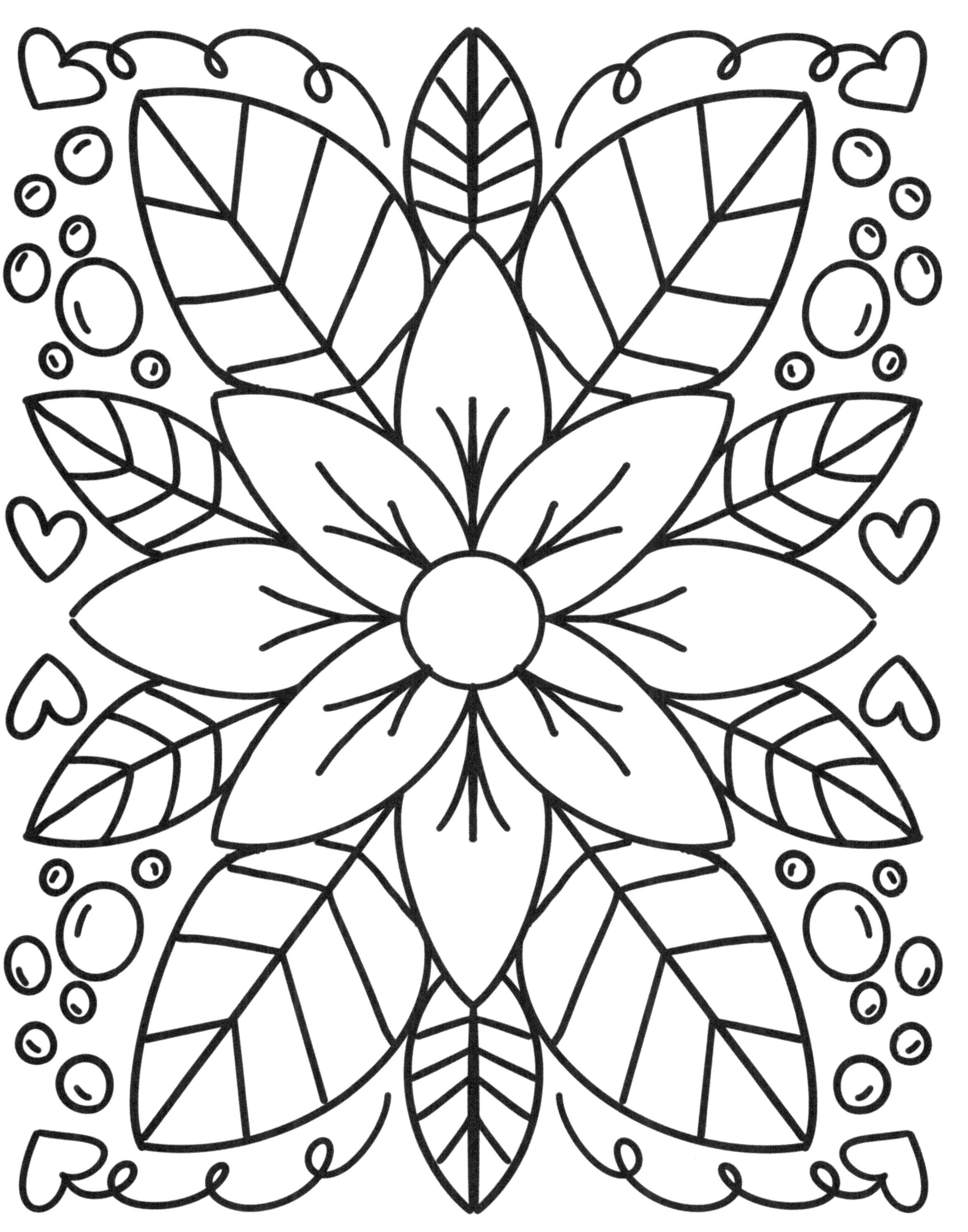

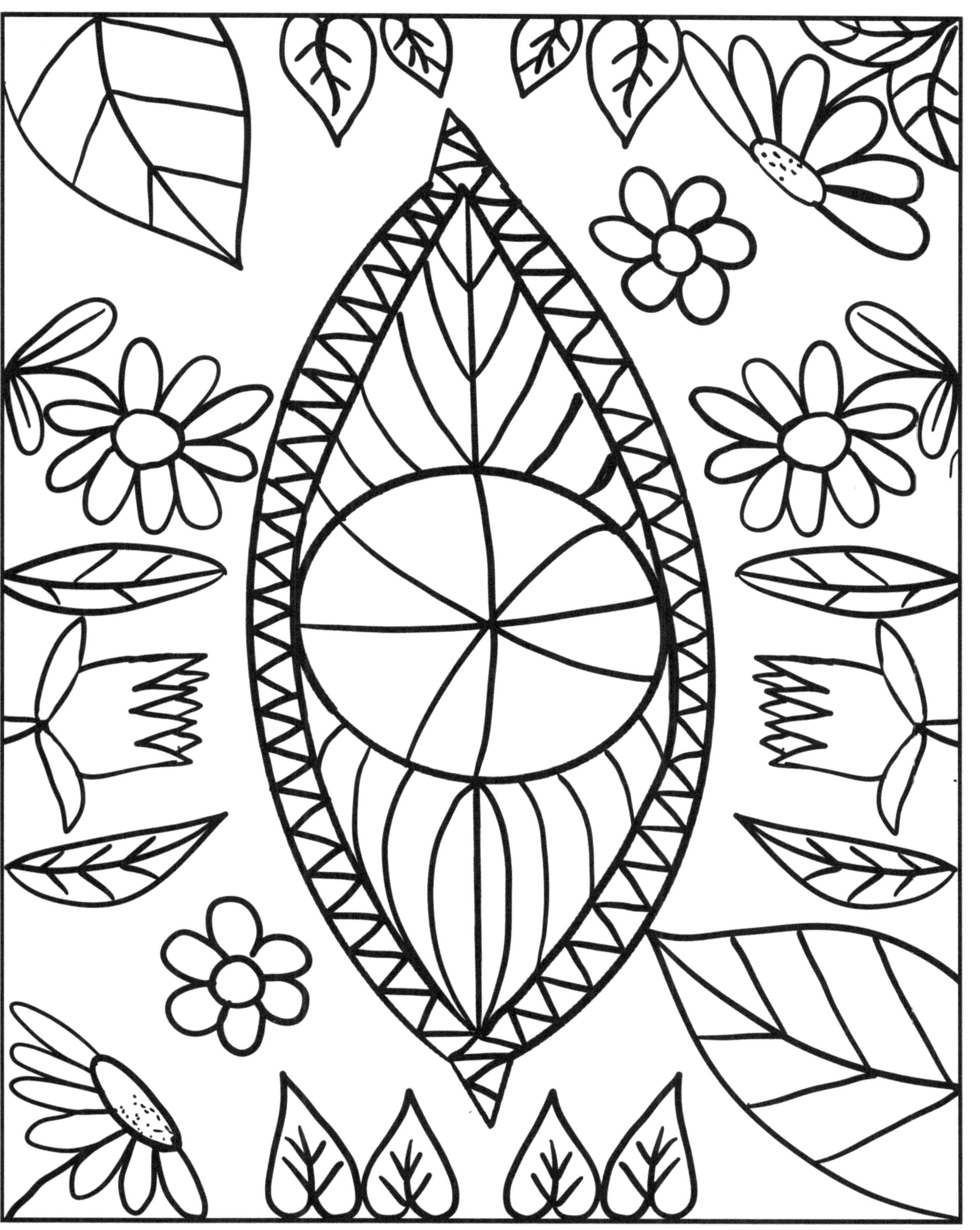

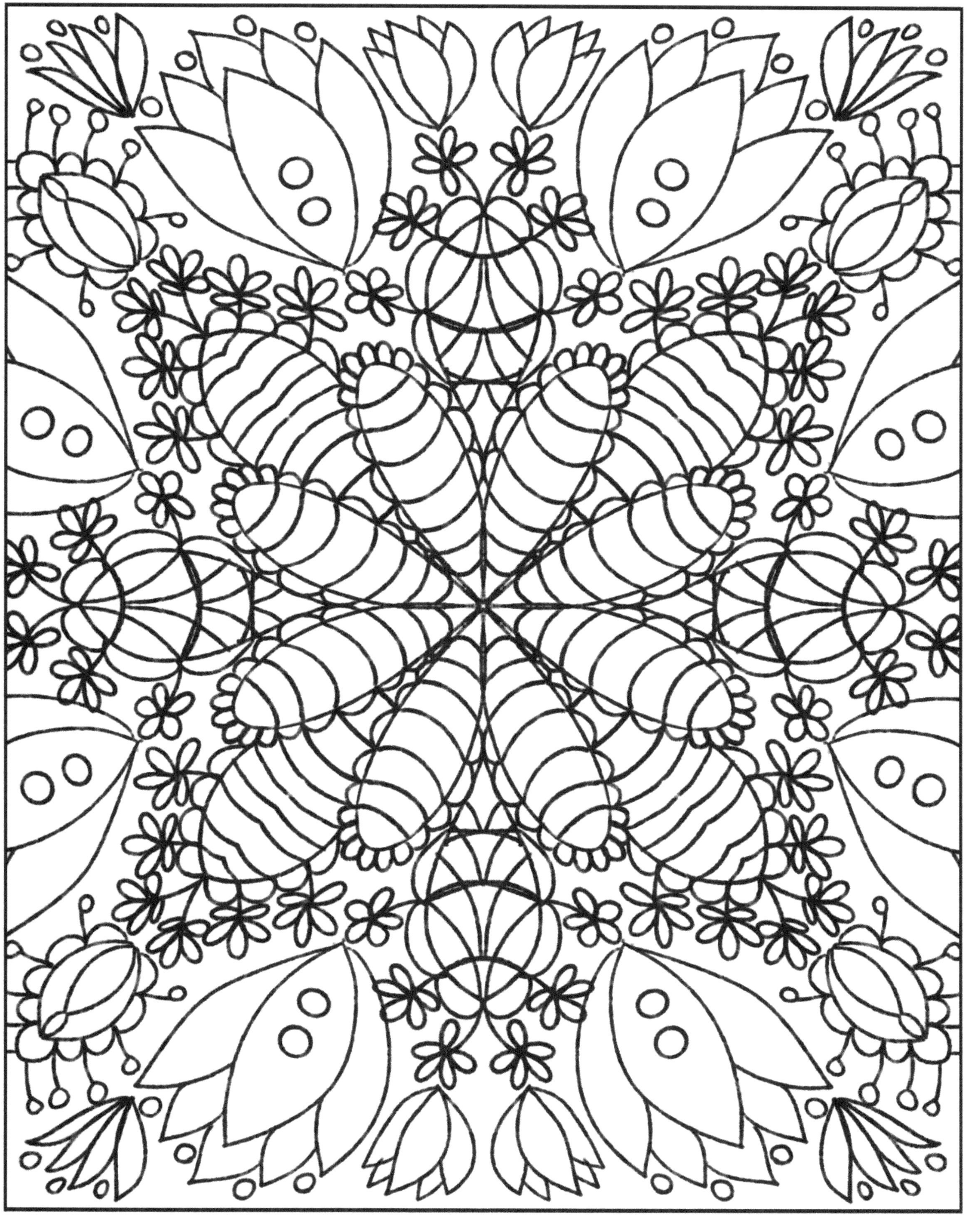

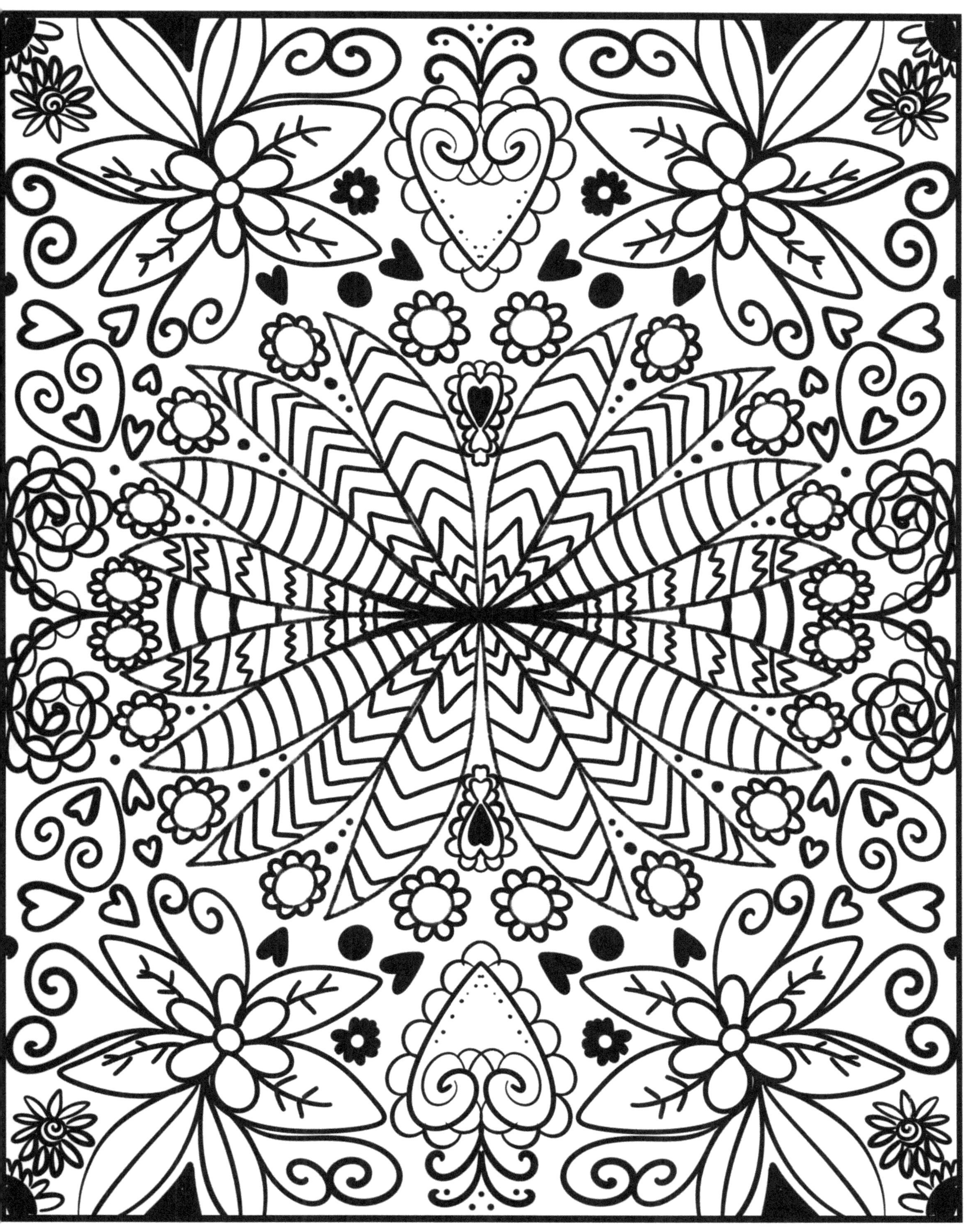

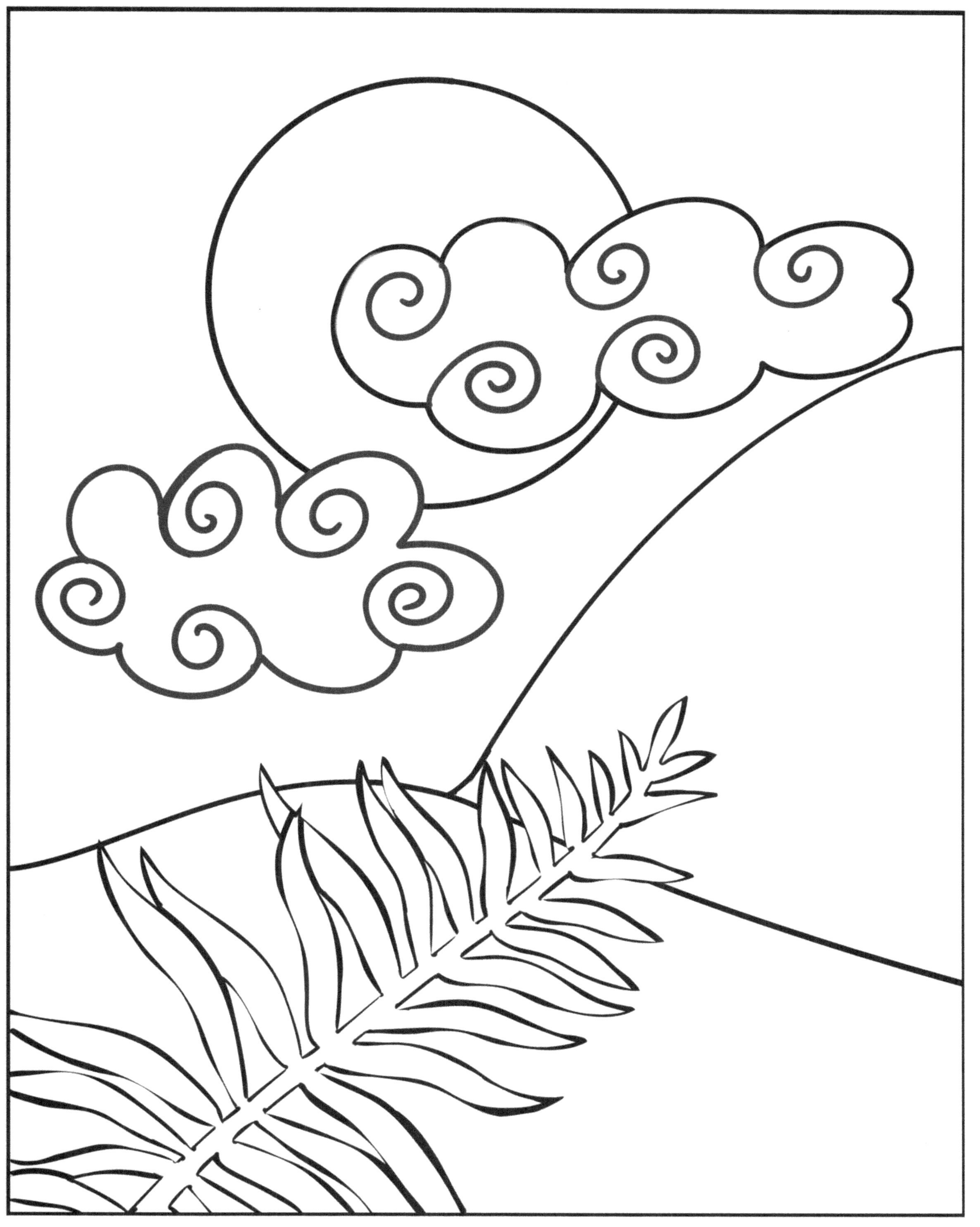

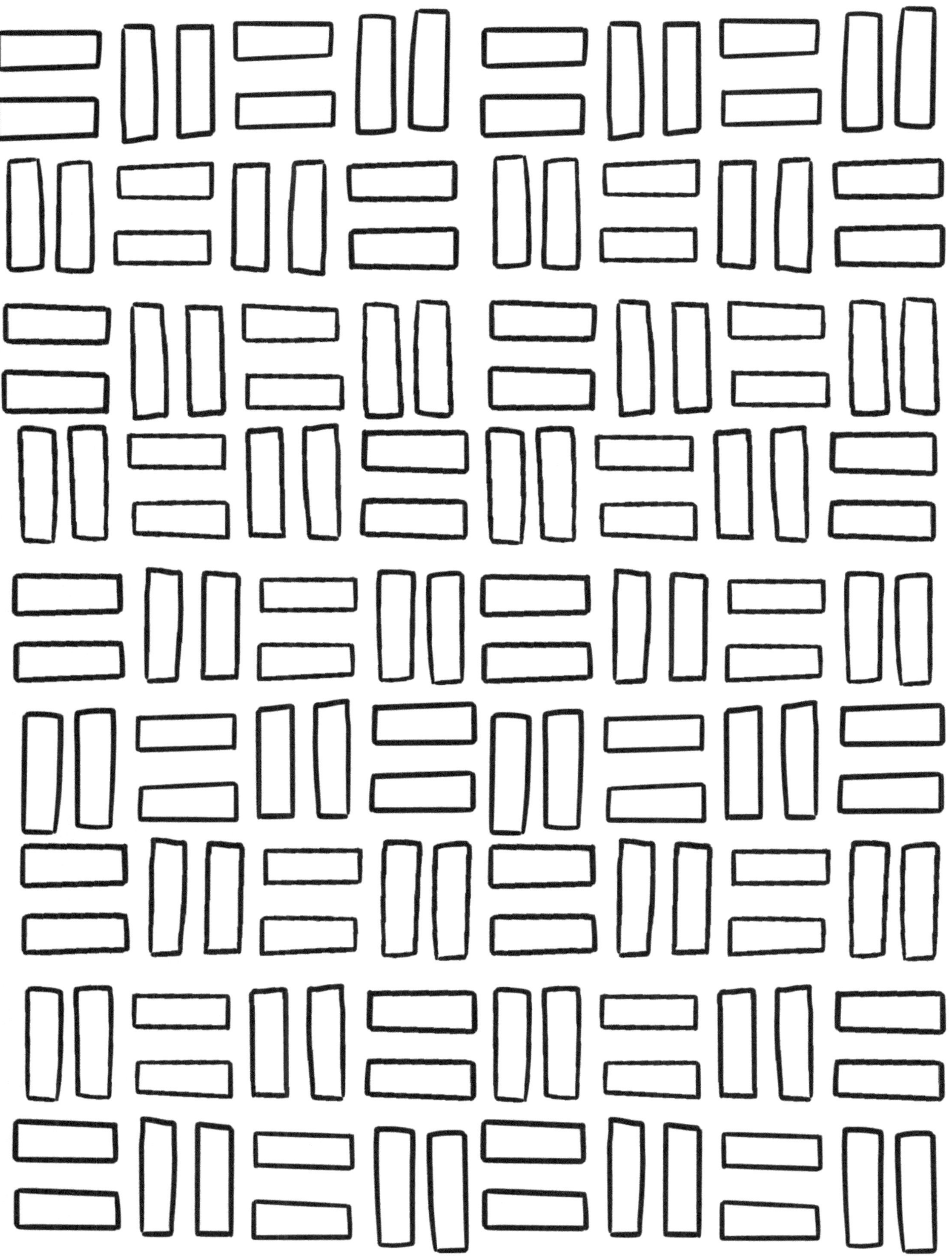

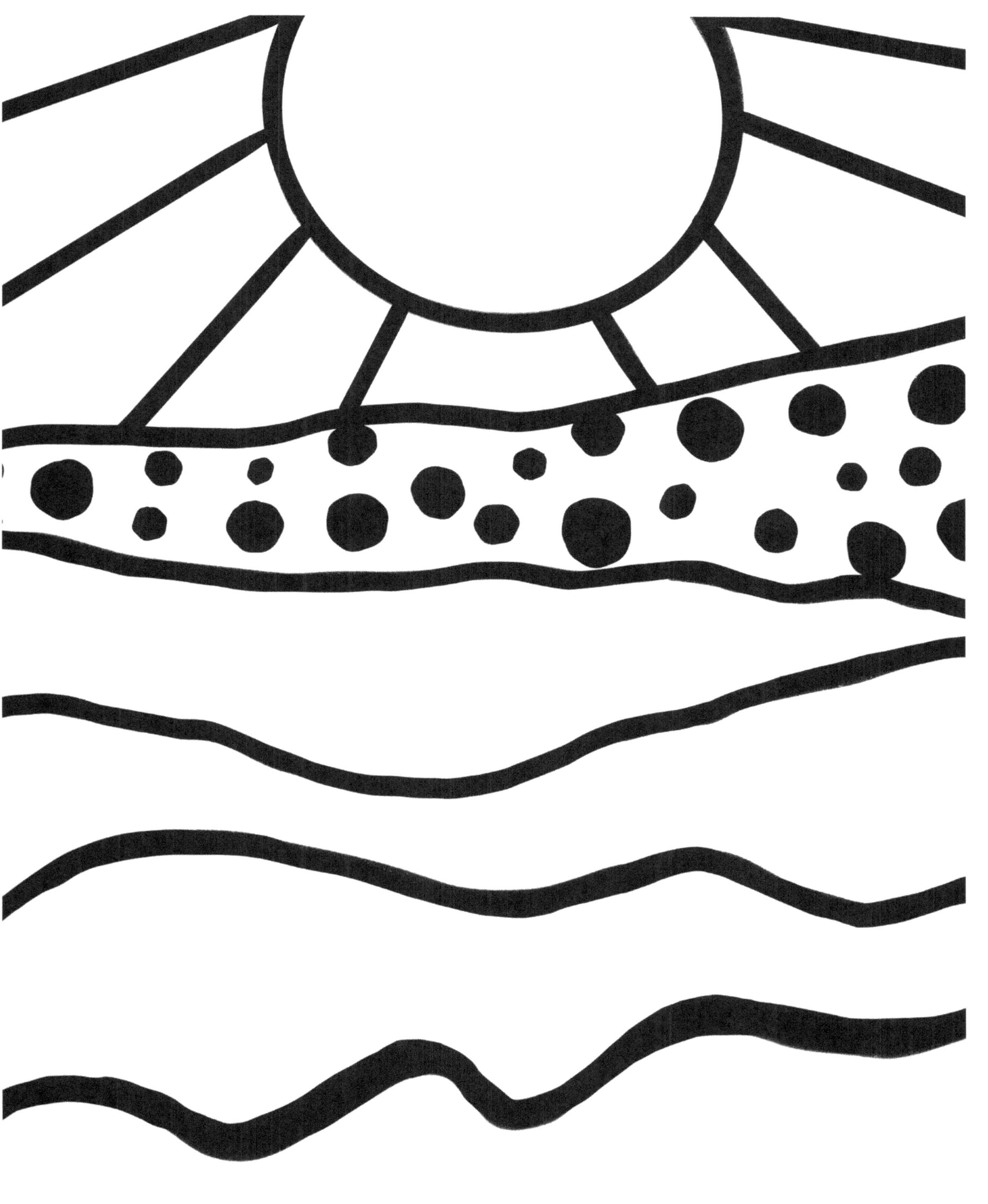

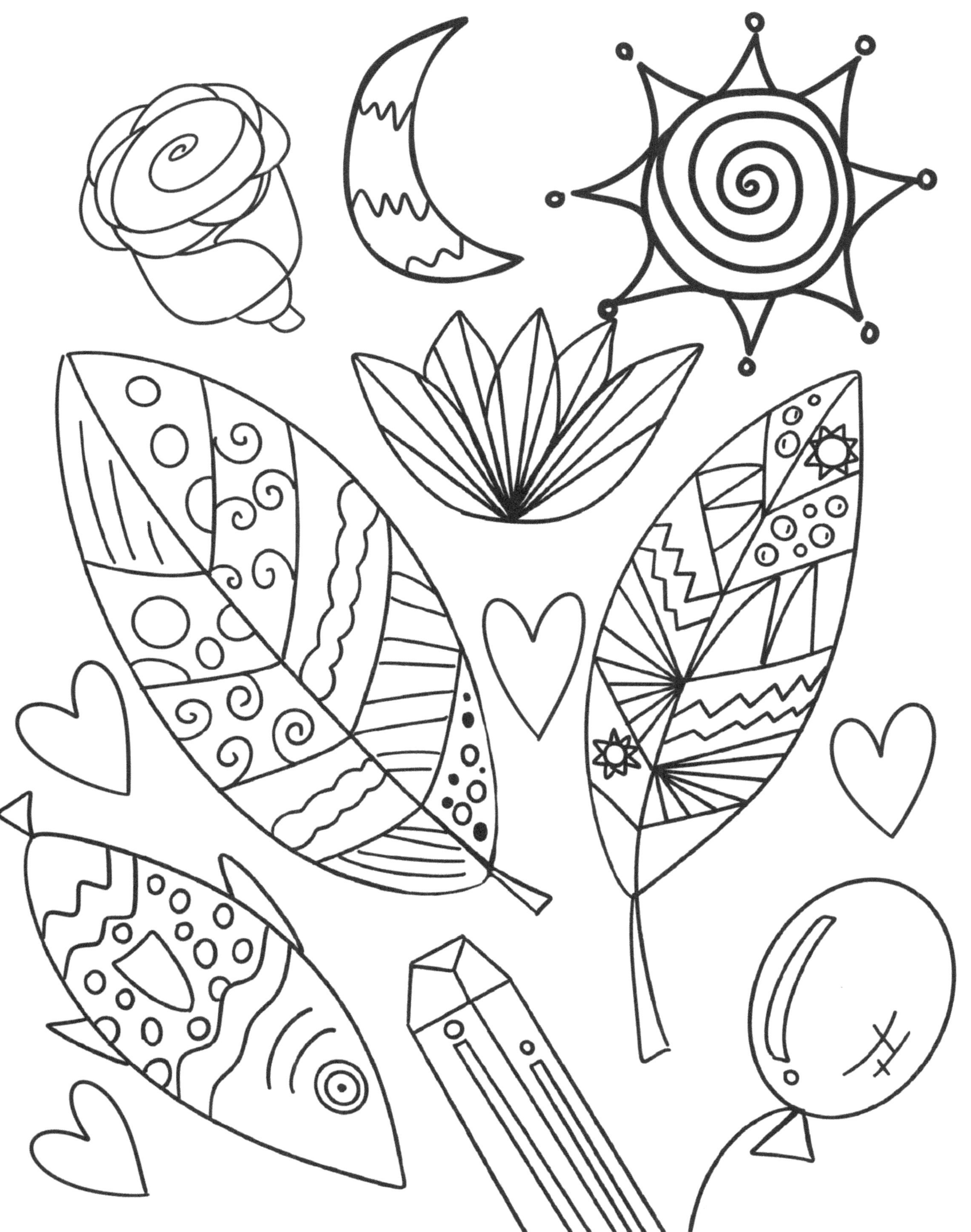

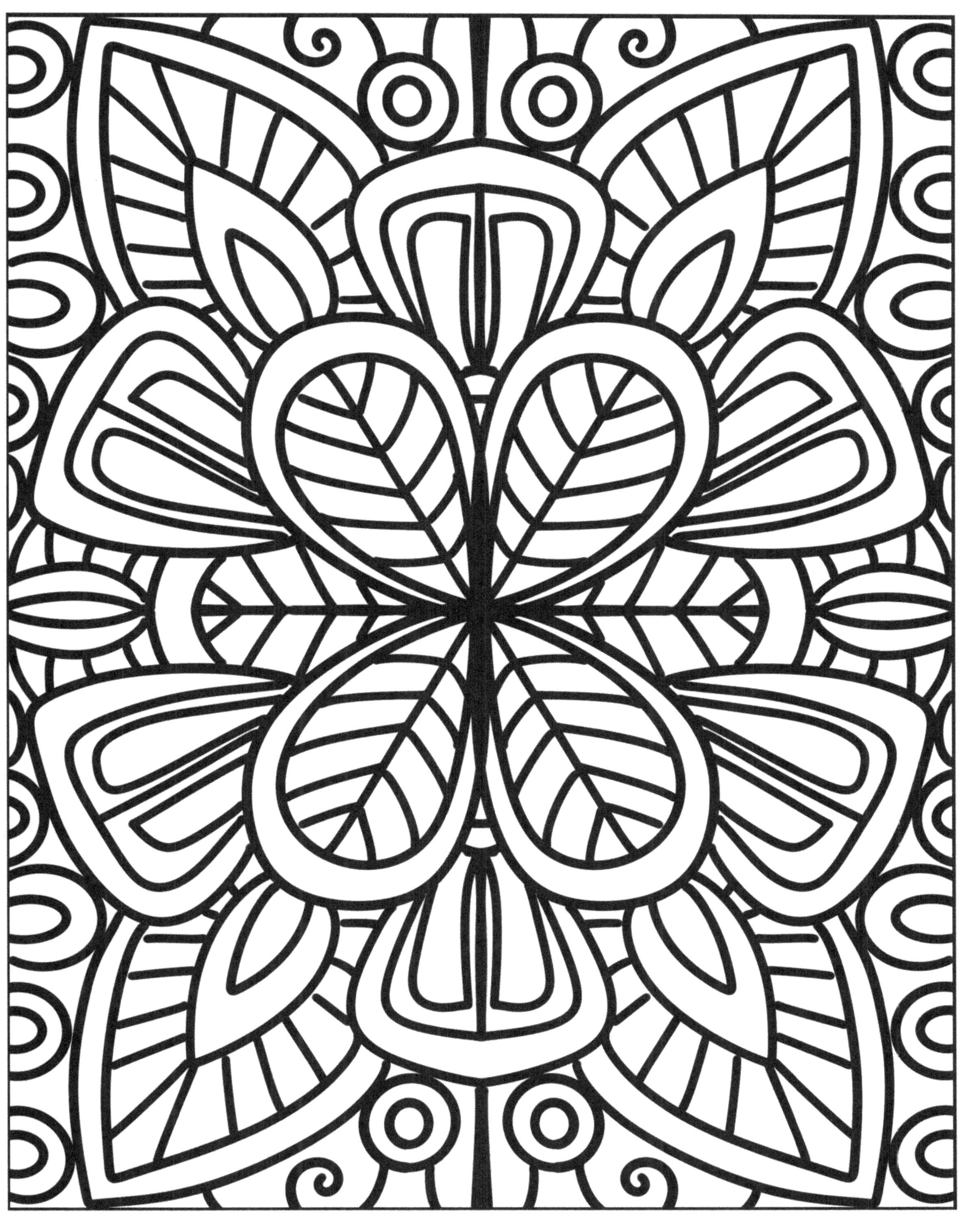

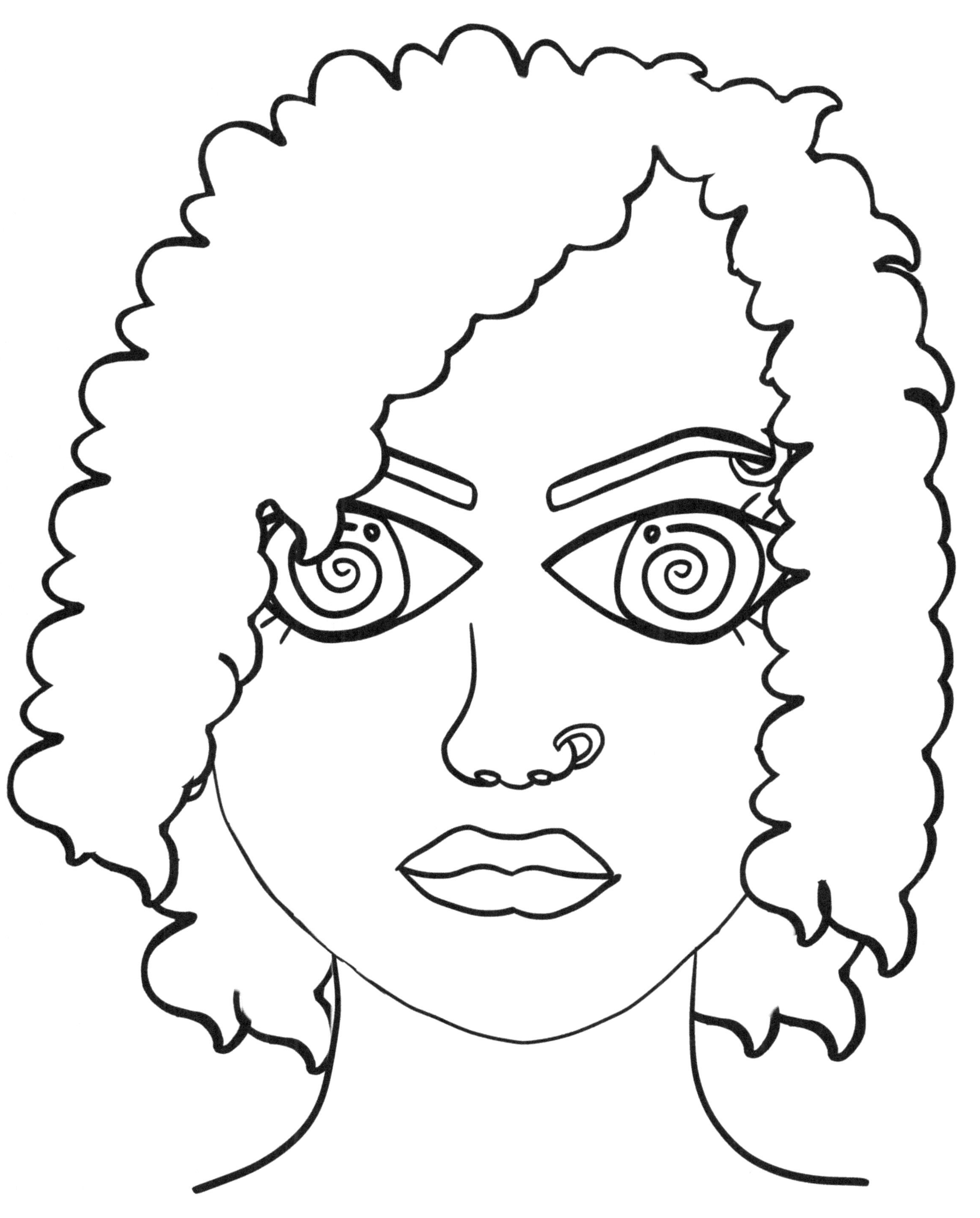

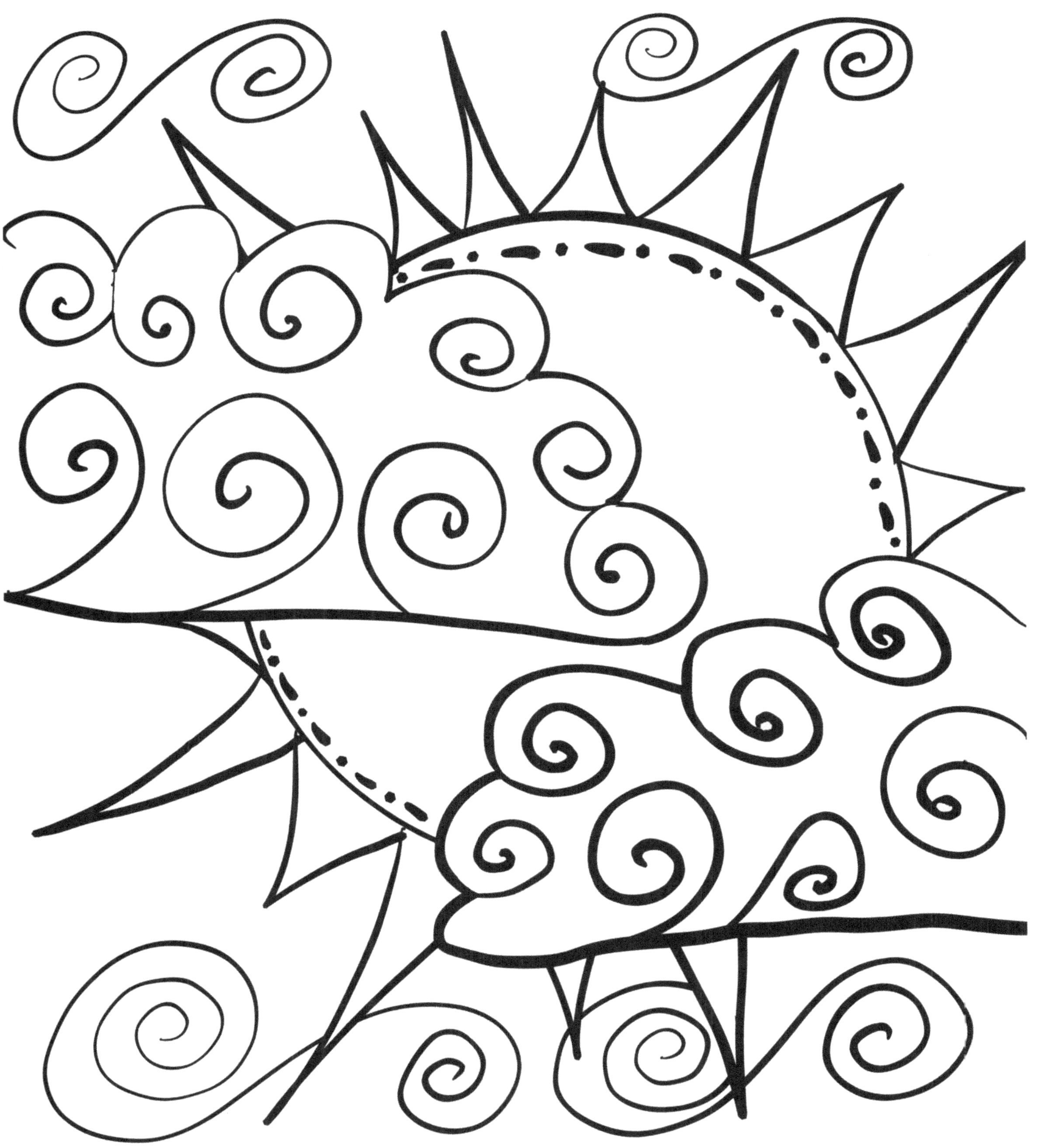

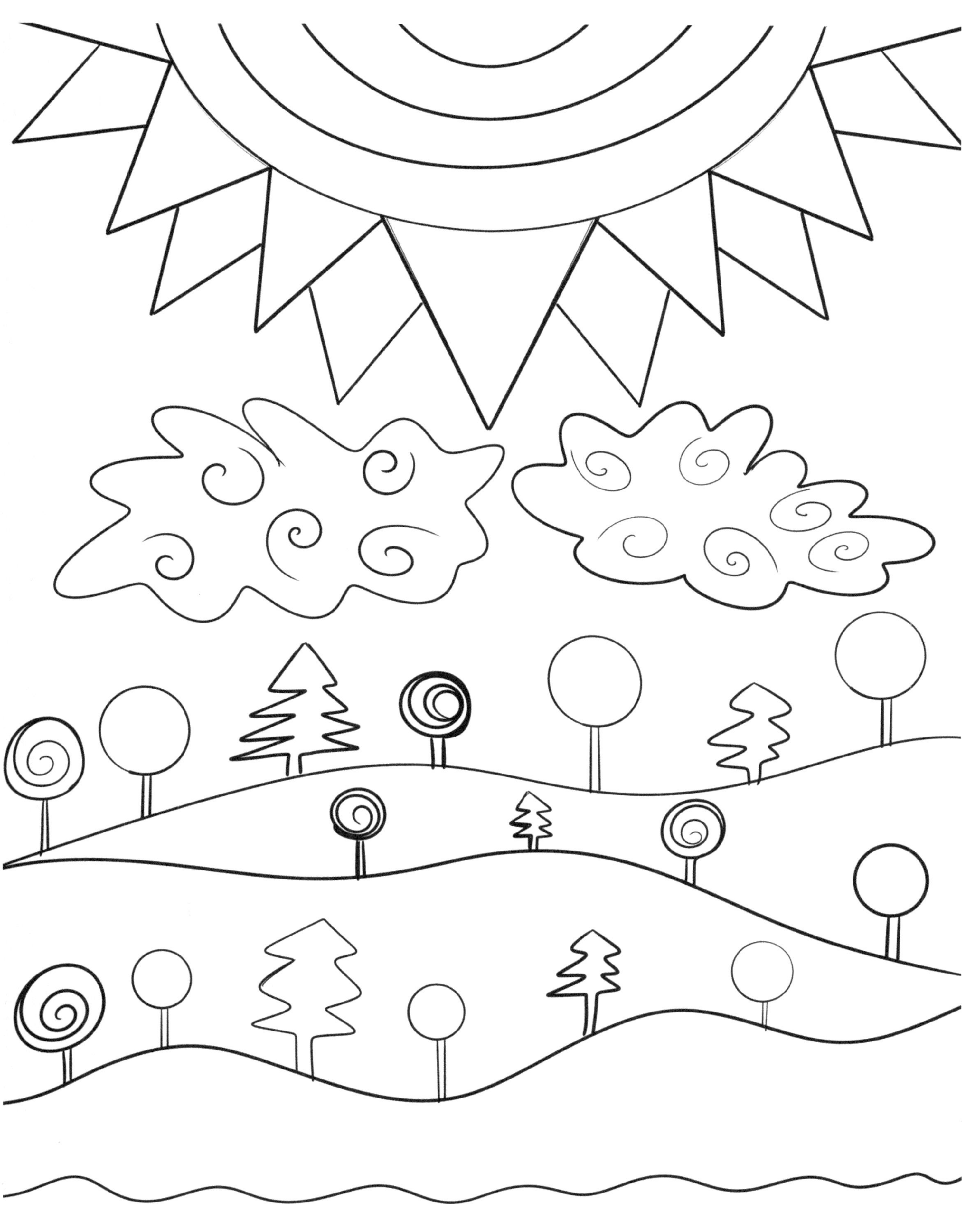

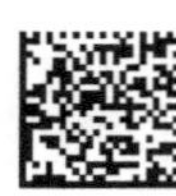